"Engh has given us a gift. This book lays out the power and promise of congregation-based community organizing generally, and more specifically amplifies the voices of scores of inspirational women from the Bible to the present who are role models for all of us. Every person who yearns to see faith communities transform our world into being more just should read this book."—**Rabbi Jonah Pesner**, Religious Action Center of Reform Judaism

"Engh's book is a treasure trove of practical wisdom, centering the transformational experience of women. It is an extraordinary, eye-opening, soul-feeding, deeply insightful, splendidly practical guide to engaging the arts of community organizing as spiritual practice for the sake of more equitable and life-giving congregations, communities, and societies. This book is a must-read for those who hunger to cultivate vibrant faith communities that link spirituality with public engagement to address the causes of suffering in our world today. Engh's voice is charged with grace, and will evoke active hope and results where powerlessness or stagnation have seeped in. The Holy Spirit is at work in this book. May it be read avidly by congregational and denominational leaders, professors and students, community organizers, and all who seek to embody God's justice-making love in this world."—**Cynthia Moe-Lobeda**, Pacific Lutheran Theological Seminary

"Engh brings a fresh and needed vision to faith-based organizing from the vantage point of a woman whose work for justice seeks to transform organizing culture itself. She shares insight and stories from her own experiences that illustrate tried and true organizing tools, while challenging leaders to reevaluate assumptions tied to gender and race that undermine true relational power. Engh presents the stories of Biblical women in conversation with the diverse voices and witness of women leaders organizing today. This book opens a critical way forward for justice work in these days."—**Rev. Heidi Neumark**, Trinity Lutheran Church of Manhattan

"The power of Engh's excellent book is in the interweaving of women's voices and experiences. From biblical foremothers to present leaders these voices tell a story of struggle, freedom, dignity and power. They also reveal the very concrete relational arts of community organizing, how leaders are formed, how a bottom line commitment to powerful leaders and powerful communities can transform God's world. It has been my privilege to have

known and walked with some of the women in this book. Engh has knit together these individual narratives into a powerful picture of a transforming vision for the church and the world. She is not naïve about the challenges of this organizing work, or the continuing challenges faced by women who take up this vocation. But her hope and faith shine through and inspire us all."—
Rev. Stephen Bouman, Evangelical Lutheran Church in America

Women's Work

Women's Work

The Transformational Power of Faith-Based Community Organizing

Susan L. Engh

LEXINGTON BOOKS/FORTRESS ACADEMIC
Lanham • Boulder • New York • London

Published by Lexington Books/Fortress Academic

Lexington Books is an imprint of The Rowman & Littlefield Publishing Group, Inc.
4501 Forbes Boulevard, Suite 200, Lanham, Maryland 20706
www.rowman.com

6 Tinworth Street, London SE11 5AL

British Library Cataloguing in Publication Information Available

Library of Congress Cataloging-in-Publication Data Available

Names: Engh, Susan, author.
Title: Women's work : the transformational power of faith-based community
    organizing / Susan Engh.
Description: Lanham : Lexington Books-Fortress Academic, 2019. | Includes
    bibliographical references and index.
Identifiers: LCCN 2018054659 (print) | LCCN 2019003408 (ebook) | ISBN
    9781978706316 (Electronic) | ISBN 9781978706309 (cloth)
    ISBN 9781978706323 (pbk)
Subjects: LCSH: Women in church work. | Religious institutions.
Classification: LCC BV4415 (ebook) | LCC BV4415 .E54 2019 (print) | DDC
    267/.4—dc23

LC record available at https://lccn.loc.gov/2018054659

Dedicated to
Bianca Vazquez, Kristen Kane,
and Meghan Sobocienski,
and in memory of
John I. Norton

Contents

Contents

Table and Figure

Acknowledgments

I wish to thank the twenty-one women interviewed for this book, each of whom courageously and generously authorized the use of her words as illustrations of the book's topics. Your power and bold leadership continue to inspire me, and add incredible depth and legitimacy to this work!

Unless otherwise noted, scripture quotations are from New Revised Standard Version Bible, copyright © 1989 National Council of the Churches of Christ in the United States of America. Used by permission. All rights reserved.

A website accompanying this book, including a study guide and a link to contact the author, is at www.womenswork.faith.

Foreword

Kim Bobo

My dear friend and organizer extraordinaire, Heather Booth, began organizing on civil rights while in high school. In college at the University of Chicago, she organized on civil rights and women's issues. After college, with two young children, she joined with some friends to fight for more childcare options in the Hyde Park neighborhood and eventually established a city-wide childcare advocacy organization.

During this childcare organizing, she attended her first official organizing training in Chicago. Although Heather says she learned a lot from the training, the trainers questioned why she was organizing on childcare issues. They belittled her in the evaluation session until she cried. The few women present weren't encouraged to be organizers.

Nevertheless, Heather kept organizing. After getting fired for organizing women clerical workers, she filed a suit and won. With the money won from the suit, she established a training center, Midwest Academy, that affirmed women as organizers.

Over the years, as the Reverend Susan Engh explains, the faith-based organizing networks changed their approaches. They learned that women not only made great leaders in their organizations, they made great organizers.

Reverend Engh's book, which you hold in your hands, offers insights into the power of faith-based organizing in changing and empowering women, as well as the amazing contributions women are making to faith-based community organizations. She offers concrete ways in which faith-based community organizing brings energy and focus to congregations, communities, and denominations.

As someone who has worked in the faith-based organizing and advocacy world for forty years (we won't add up how old that makes me!), I have certainly seen many changes over the years in how women organizers and leaders are recruited, mentored, trained, promoted, and supported, but there are still challenges to tapping the full potential of women leaders and organizers. Let me applaud the approach of this book and suggest a few thoughts from my own experience about how we might do more to develop and support future organizers—both women and men.

We must welcome and respect new women organizers. About ten years ago, I sent one of my summer interns to meet with a legendary organizer. He treated her like dirt. He asked why she thought she could do any organizing. She left convinced that she never wanted to work with organizers again.

As a young faith-based organizer, I experienced a fair amount of this myself. When I first began organizing, there was a group of mostly older white guys who were "the organizing folks" in the denominational world. I tried to meet with them and build a relationship. I was not given the time of day. Years later, when I moved to Chicago and had ten years of organizing experience under my belt, I was asked the same question as my intern by a veteran faith-based organizer: "Why do you think you can do organizing?"

There has been a school of thought in organizing that this sort of tough treatment pushes people to stand up for themselves. Perhaps it does—sometimes. But many times, it just turns off people, especially women and young people, needlessly. We don't need to treat people disrespectfully. It doesn't build the base of organizers. We need the skills and talents of young organizers and certainly the skills and talents of women. This book highlights the power women bring to organizing in both the secular and faith communities. Young organizers and women are teaching us how to do things in new ways. We need to be welcoming and to encourage the engagement of as many new, young and women organizers as possible.

We must encourage and guide young organizers. I've worked with lots of young organizers over the years. Although organizing is clearly not suited for everyone, there are lots of potentially marvelous organizers who give up too early because they haven't gotten adequate support and encouragement.

Most of us starting out in our careers are insecure. We don't have the experience necessary to develop self-confidence. Over the years, I've observed that young men organizers and young women organizers express their insecurities in fairly different ways. Young men often boast and bluster and talk as if they can do anything. They talk too much in meetings and don't ask for enough help. Young women, on the other hand, will often talk about how terrified they are to speak in public or how unsure they are in new situations. They will often hold back in meetings, feeling they have little to offer. Although not all young men or young women behave in these ways, I have seen these differences repeatedly over the years. I think some of my older male

colleagues in the organizing world have seen the young men as more qualified, because they behave as if they are less insecure. Rather, these are culturally produced ways of operating. If women organizers are to be nurtured
and developed, we must not mistake their insecurities (which their male peers
often share, even if they don't express them in the same way!) as insurmount-
able barriers. They simply need experience.

One young woman organizer working for me was a classic example. She
confessed to me that she was terrified to speak in public. She was happy to
do the behind-the-scenes work but didn't want to be out front. One day my
office got a call about a group of Latino workers who hadn't been paid and
were furious. They were meeting at a nearby local church with church and
community leaders and wanted our help to figure out what to do. I couldn't
go. I called a few other organizers to go help facilitate the meeting, but no one
could make it. I asked this young woman to go, translate between groups, and
help them develop a plan. She was terrified. We talked through the meeting
and how to handle things. I coached her on pretending to be self-confident
even if she didn't feel it. And I assured her that she didn't need to be perfect
and that good things would come out of her work. And they did. She helped
the workers develop a plan. She got English- and Spanish-speaking people
listening to one another. She stood with the workers as they got their money
back. She was awesome. That evening, she began the confidence-building
track that made her a great organizer.

We must change the macho talk. The organizing world, including the faith-
based organizing world, is known for its tough and aggressive manner of
talking (and sometimes behaving). People can be challenged to grow and be
a strong leader without being yelled at or embarrassed in public settings—or
made to cry, like Heather. In Reverend Engh's own story, she shows the
power of being challenged, but relates how this can be done without bully-
ing and hurting people. Yes, we must be tough and clear on our strategies
and willing to take risks in our tactics and approaches, but we can be strong
and powerful without using language that people, especially women, find
offensive. As more women become leaders in the organizing world, this is
changing, but over the years, macho talk has been a turn-off for many women
organizers, as well as normal people whom we want to organize.

We must create more family-friendly jobs. One reason so many organizing
jobs were held by men was that in the recent past, the organizing lifestyles
were impossible for women, especially women with young (or nursing) children. Union organizers would be sent to communities and live in hotels for
weeks on end. Community organizers were expected to meet with leaders
every evening and then drink with fellow organizers to "debrief" late into the
night. Although faith-based community organizers' lifestyles were slightly

better than those of union or community organizers, they were still grueling for most women with families.

A few years ago, a dear clergy friend, who is a phenomenal organizer, told me she felt like she had to choose between organizing and having a family. She wanted to have children but didn't see how she could do so and keep her organizing job. I told her—what I think is the truth—it will be hard, but you can do it. If we want more women organizers (and many men, too), we need to figure out how to make these jobs more accommodating for people with kids and families. We can figure out how to offer more flexible hours or give maternity or paternity leave or allow moms to bring their nursing children to work.

We must nurture our faith and spirituality. Organizing is hard. The path to winning real victories or building fabulous leaders is never crystal-clear. Sometimes it is hard to see the results in the short term. Many times, we are short on money or people to do the work as well as we'd like. And the work is never finished.

Even though faith-based organizers are around congregations and people of faith all the time, we still must be intentional to nurture our own religious beliefs and spiritual practices. Once I had a woman organizer working for me who, despite having graduated from seminary and working in a faith-based organization, had not been to church for almost two years. She was overly critical of everyone around her, published harsh and attacking words on Facebook, and always felt burned out. Although there were probably many things going on in this woman's life, she was not nurturing her inner being.

Nurturing our own spirits helps us forgive ourselves and others, centers us so we control what we say and how we say it (as opposed to flying off the handle), and allows us to have hope during challenging situations. All of us, but especially those organizing within faith communities, must nurture our private selves. We must remember what draws us to the work and nurture those values and relationships with powers greater than ourselves.

We must learn and celebrate the history of organizing. People of faith have organized since the beginning of time, as Reverend Engh illustrates through all her fabulous biblical stories of organizing. What we are doing through faith-based organizing and advocacy is not new. We are building on the work of those who came before us—powerful men and women of all races and backgrounds. We are truly standing on the shoulders of saints. This book provides one way for organizers to learn the history of organizing, including through biblical stories, through examples of success, and through women's stories. We hear the words of ancient and modern-day saints.

It's hard to imagine a time more in need of organizing and organizers than right now. I'm confident this book will add to our knowledge, strengthen the field, and encourage new organizers. Thank you, Reverend Engh, for this contribution.

Introduction

THE CONGREGATION'S
RELATIONSHIP TO ITS COMMUNITY

Leaders and members of religious congregations that want to move beyond their proverbial four walls and out into their communities of context have several choices for how to do so. Those compelled by their faith traditions and sacred texts to "do good" in the world around them—and not simply to draw others into their own spaces, rituals, and faith-oriented activities—might choose charitable work, addressing the immediate needs of others. Or congregations can get involved in community development, investing in and accompanying people in ways that increase their capacity to meet their own needs into the future. Another way congregations sometimes engage with the public sphere is through advocacy. At its root, the term means to speak on behalf of someone else. So those who advocate speak out about issues or policies that are negatively affecting certain sectors in their community, appealing for change to those who have the power to alter the situation.

More and more religious congregations in the United States are choosing yet another way to foster change for the sake of building a more just society. Faith-based community organizing looks at the systems, policies, attitudes, and practices that contribute to inequities in place between populations in any given community. It focuses on building relationships and affinities between people with varying levels of power and influence. It trains leaders to take collective action on their own and others' behalf, in order to change the very systems that perpetuate injustice. Faith-based community organizing rarely concerns itself with charitable activities. Occasionally it delves into community development. Often it uses the tactics of advocacy. But it adds the important distinctions of intentional leadership development, the building of collective power through deep relational investment, and taking collective, decisive, public action to catalyze the needed changes identified by its participants.

WOMEN'S TESTIMONY

Like much of what happens in religious organizations, women are active participants and leaders in the realm of faith-based community organizing. However, very little has been written by or about women in organizing; about their own development, about their unique struggles, about the significant contributions they make. This book intends to remedy that deficit. I aim to show that, through their engagement in this field, women experience liberative transformation, both personally and professionally. Further, through their actions and leadership, women who embrace organizing are catalysts of significant transformation in their congregations, faith traditions, organizations, and communities.

In researching this book, I interviewed twenty-one women in an attempt to represent the diversity of voices of those active in the field. Many of them I know from my own career in organizing. I was introduced to others by mutual acquaintances and only met them when I interviewed them for this book. Some important voices are missing from this collection, notably more women active in the DART organization and high-level staff members from the Industrial Areas Foundation. For various reasons, including some women's unavailability for interviews within my given timeframe, I could not fully cover the range of networks and diversity of women active in the field. However, I believe the experiences of the women who are included to be amply wide-ranging, representative, trustworthy, and inspiring.

Through the accounts of these twenty-one women, and through my framing of their and my own experiences in organizing, I will bring women's testimony forward in order to stir interest and instruct people about the field of faith-based community organizing. In this regard, the book can serve as a primer on this type of organizing, with the experience of women as its illustrative theme. My hope is that, by learning these stories and understanding these concepts, more congregations and leaders (women and men) will be motivated to enter into this realm of ministry and contribute to the furthering of divine justice in the world.

HOW IT BEGAN FOR ME

I sat in a classroom full of clergy, thirty-five to forty in number, from a variety of faith traditions: Black, White, Latino; mostly men. I was one of the few women. We had come together for three days, from our respective ministries across the country, as part of the Gamaliel community organizing network's National Clergy Caucus annual gathering. It was my first time.

This session was the only one at the event that was considered actual training. The other sessions, led by the clergy themselves, were presentations, sharing of best practices, break-out time in affinity groups, theological explorations, and so on. Highly informative, relational and inspirational, but certainly not confrontational. Gamaliel's most respected and seasoned trainer, Mary Gonzales, was to lead this particular session. Mary is a tall, physically imposing Latina who exudes confidence and commands the room. I had not encountered her before.

Mary began to work the space, moving up and down the aisles, frequently leaning in close to address individual participants. She combined the teaching of content with an aggressive Socratic method, engaging and confronting participants one at a time and all at once. The tension in the room grew palpable, as each person anticipated being her next subject of attention.

As I watched and waited, vicariously impacted by Mary's challenges to my peers, I was aware of a growing excitement in my belly, a quickening of my heart rate, a rising flush to my face. I simultaneously hoped and feared that she would come my way and address me directly. When she eventually did, I remember setting down my pen to face her, smiling warily. She began her engagement with me by saying, "You've been awfully quiet, Reverend. What's going on for you?" As she worked me over for the next several minutes, I remember thinking that I had never before been taken so seriously by someone who didn't know me! I remember feeling, as a result of the encounter, convicted yet affirmed, challenged yet accepted, judged yet validated.

Later I would learn that the style of training Mary so capably demonstrated is called agitation. I would experience it again and again from Gamaliel trainers in the coming years. And, starting with Mary's session at that clergy gathering, I would be transformed by it and by those who courageously practice it. I also would learn that not everyone in that room with me that day, or in other training sessions, appreciates the agitational approach. But I have come to believe that it is the most effective relational tool for moving a person from where they are to where they need to be. By daring to agitate me and others to be transformed into the leaders God intends for us to be, those who practice it exhibit one of the most powerful forms of love that I know.

A QUICK TOUR OF THIS BOOK

This book is about women and transformation through faith-based community organizing: transformation of the kind I've described above, in which women experience it personally or professionally; and transformation that women make happen through their own actions and leadership. Each chapter includes extensive quotes from the women I interviewed, in order for readers to truly know their stories and not just hear of them through someone else's interpretation.

Each chapter begins with my own analysis of a story about a "foremother in faith" from the Bible—a key resource for organizing in my own Christian tradition. Each of these biblical figures, I suggest, was transformed and transformational, many of them, whether knowingly or not, employing the tools of organizing. Reinterpreting these women's stories through the lens of transformed and transformational women of power has been important in my own formation as a leader. I include them here in honor of their rightful roles in history and in my own journey, and as a further lifting up of voices and stories that often have been misinterpreted or neglected altogether. Readers whose own faith traditions are different from my own may not identify immediately with these figures, but may still find these examples instructive, and I encourage a thorough reexamination of women from one's own sacred texts or traditions, if and as that process is meaningful.

Chapter 1, "The Transformation of Women," examines how their engagement with faith-based community organizing often fosters profound personal and professional changes for women. There is conventional wisdom in the phrase "transformed women transform." Although someone might enter into this field with the main purpose of gaining tools and skills for making a difference in one's community, it almost invariably begins with the woman herself being transformed.

Chapter 2 deals with "The Transformation of Local Faith Communities." Community organizers, from Saul Alinsky (often considered the "father of community organizing" in the United States) to the present day, have recruited religious congregations mainly under the practical strategy of "organizing the organized." They can gain a significant base of leaders and financial resources all at once by bringing a congregation (rather than individuals) into this work. What organizers too seldom focus on is the opportunity for whole congregations to be transformed by participating. But it can and does happen, and women play a key role, as their stories illustrate.

In chapter 3, "The Transformation of National Religious Bodies," I examine how certain faith traditions in the United States have so embraced the principles and practices of community organizing that the character of those institutions has been transformed. In each case, women have played a central and intentional role in this transformation. Five key examples are shared.

Chapter 4, "The Transformation of Community Organizations," looks at the role women have played in the development, growth, and ongoing trans-

formation of the faith-based community organizing networks in the
States. DART, Gamaliel, the Industrial Areas Foundation, and PICO
Faith in Action) were founded, and directed for most of their history,
White men. Only recently has the first woman, also the first person of color,
taken on the role of executive director of one of the networks, Gamaliel. But
women have been on the scene in each of the networks from the very start,
spearheading organizational formation and change. Some of their stories,
shared here, illustrate how this has taken place.

Chapter 5 lifts up the stories of how women have contributed to "The
Transformation of Communities." A shared vision among practitioners in the
field of faith-based community organizing is that neighborhoods, wider communities, even the culture itself, will be transformed by this work. We start by
understanding and working within "the world as it is," but we always strive
for "the world as it should be." For people of faith, the latter is inextricably
tied to "the world as God intends it to be." This kind of transformation usually
happens incrementally, sometimes only provisionally, yet often quite profoundly, as leaders and organizations take on issues whose outcomes produce
greater equity and justice. Women contribute significantly to these transfor-
mations, as you will come to understand through the stories these women tell.

In chapter 6, "Women's Paths to Power," I revisit each of the women we
have already met throughout this book. What we experience here is a deeper
dive into the motivations and personal histories of each woman that led her to
engage with faith-based community organizing. Chapter 6 concludes with a
series of probing questions, to challenge the reader into deeper self-reflection
and action.

Chapter One

The Transformation of Women

"Sir, give me this [living] water, so that I may never be thirsty or have to keep coming here to draw water." (John 4:15)

THE WOMAN AT THE WELL:
FROM OUTCAST TO EVANGELIST

In the New Testament, in the fourth chapter of the Gospel of John, is the story of an unnamed Samaritan woman whom Jesus meets at a well on the outskirts of her village (John 4:3–42). Jesus, tired out from his journey from Judea to Galilee, is sitting alone by the well when the woman comes there, also alone, to draw water. We learn that their meeting is a cultural taboo; unrelated women and men were not permitted to converse, and certainly not while unchaperoned. Further, Samaritans were the historical enemies of Jews, whom they considered unclean heretics.

Early in their exchange, the woman points out both of these cultural dynamics, questioning Jesus' defiance of these factors by asking her for a drink of water. But Jesus disregards her caution and suggests that *he*, actually, is the one who can provide *her* with refreshment, with what he refers to as "living water." Her curiosity about his claim leads them into a deeply theological and personal conversation.

They discuss matters that reveal profound truths about each of them, not least of which is that Jesus is the Messiah, long-awaited by both Jews and Samaritans. For the woman, what Jesus uncovers about her—married five times and now living, unmarried, with yet another man—could have been cause for shame. But she shows no embarrassment, instead interpreting his candor and insight as prophetic.

She emerges from her encounter with Jesus transformed. Forgetting her water jar and the reason she went to the well in the first place, she returns in haste

7

to her village, excited to tell about the conversation to neighbors who would have avoided her previously because of her social status. As a result of hearing this woman's story, the villagers—Samaritans all—rush to welcome Jesus—a Jew—into their midst; and many are converted, both by the woman's testimony and by Jesus' message of salvation.

SISTERS AT THE WELL

Many women, through their participation in faith-based community organizing, experience a similar kind of transformation as the woman at the well in John's Gospel. In this chapter we will explore some of those stories and the aspects of community organizing that contribute to those transformative experiences.

> Organizing gave me a voice that I probably wouldn't have claimed otherwise. I've sometimes met up with friends that knew me in high school and they're like, "Where did you come from?!" I used to be very shy; I didn't want to speak up, because everyone could then see how dumb I was. You know, that kind of belief. But this gave me a voice and a way to say, "I don't care what you think! We're going to go forward." That's been transformative for me. And I love it! People can tell that I do, when I talk about it.
>
> —Maureen Geddes

Most of the women I interviewed for this book, regardless of how much transformation they may have *fostered* through their community organizing work, pointed to *their own transformation* as the most profound part of their experience working in this field. This might be, in part, because women often are socialized to be modest and to downplay the positive effects our actions have on the world around us. But the regular recurrence of this theme in my interviews—the personal transformation of women through their exposure to organizing—is remarkable in its own right.

My own entry into organizing is a story of personal and professional transformation, at times sudden, more often incremental. Early in my ministry, I was what some have described as a mild-mannered pastor. I was a capable worship leader, a creative preacher, an engaging Bible study teacher, a compassionate counselor, a reliable partner in ministry. But as peaceable as this approach was, I also was growing more and more restless about the injustices I saw around me that clearly didn't reflect the vision God has for the world. And, it was beginning to dawn on me that the role the church was playing in it all, under the leadership of mild-mannered pastors like me, actually might be part of the problem!

At about the time that this uncomfortable insight was dawning, I was called from my first small inner-city parish to my next, a large suburban congregation. My new pastoral portfolio included social ministry, leading this affluent but generous congregation to expand its impact on the broader community, beyond its traditional charitable activities. In my quest to lead this process, I came across faith-based community organizing. A colleague introduced me to the director of a local interfaith organizing group. Not long afterward he sent me to the Gamaliel national leadership training event for clergy that I described in my opening story of this book.

At that and subsequent trainings, and through the mentoring of local organizers, I was challenged time and again to move out of my comfort zones of church-as-usual and mild-mannered pastor. The agitational question, "did you enter the ministry just to be a people pleaser?" was put to me more than once, and it rankled me! The challenge as to whether I wanted to be nice vs. powerful and effective also haunted me. I began to understand that, in order to challenge the powers-that-be which perpetuate an unjust status quo, it is necessary to build an alternative kind of power.

Other women involved in community organizing through their faith community point to their exposure to that realm as a catalyst for transformation in other areas of their lives. Mary Gruber, a Catholic lay woman who was a leader in the same Minnesota organization where I got my start, tells about how faith-based organizing impacted her career as a nurse:

> When the job came open that I have now, I took a risk and asked my nursing leader about whether or not I could apply for it if I got enrolled in a program that would give me the credentials I'd need. It didn't follow our policy, but they said yes. There were two other candidates who already had the credentials. But I got the job offered to me, contingent on being enrolled in school. I called a girlfriend to help me identify schools in Minnesota with the program I needed. I was interviewed by Winona State in their advanced nursing program and was accepted right away.
>
> I knew I wanted that job. I was totally out of compliance from being able to apply for it. But in organizing training we learn that the rules are what you believe they are! I hadn't thought about tuition or how I was going to pay for my program. It just all happened when I took the risk. I also knew, strategically, which friend to ask for help: someone who would help me do something and take action. I also think during the interview process I was more honest about speaking the truth. I went into it saying I understood how the role was done previously, but that I saw greater needs than what were currently being addressed. If I was given the opportunity, here were some things I would do differently. I had some vision and was not just saying what I thought they wanted me to say.

Gruber is quick to point out that not all of her transformation came from the formal community organizing training she was a part of, nor from the intentional influence of others. Often it was the struggles she had to work through as a leader in the field of organizing that galvanized her transformation:

> The biggest challenges have been the disparities within the community organizations at all levels. That was the hardest part for me. Because of that, though, I'm willing to speak the truth, to myself and others. That was something I didn't always do. I was more diplomatic. I wanted to be a part of the team, accommodating or respectful of the group and not trying to assert myself or my self-interest. My development came from the scars, from the fights I had to fight. I struggled a lot not to let myself become a victim.

Doran Schrantz, who worked her way up from an organizing intern to Executive Director of ISAIAH of Minnesota, also points to the pain and struggle that characterized her transformation and progress in this work:

> My first several months as an organizer were very tumultuous. I did a lot of crying. It was good for me. It was consuming. I was feeling things getting burned off me, like this thing about my deference to authority and where that came from. There was a lot of internal reflection. Organizing gave me a set of practices to move myself into a new way of being. It was painful but necessary. Every day I was doing a publicly risky thing for which I could be judged unworthy, which was my biggest fear. But it was great!

DEVELOPING POWERFUL LEADERS

> What's good about having an organization where everyone is in it to grow, you're not focused on "How do we win this campaign?" but rather "How do we build power together?" The issue campaign is a tool to do that, but it's not the end goal. That's a very different focus. When leaders say, "I demand that you invest in me," that's a very different kind of relationship.
>
> —Pamela Twiss

In community organizing, the commitment to developing leaders is at least as important as the issues that we engage. This is both a sacred priority and a practical one. From a faith perspective, this priority honors the ancient Hebrew call to pass on to each generation the ability to meet the high expectations God has for God's people: "You shall love the Lord your God with all your heart, and with all your soul, and with all your might. Keep these words that I am commanding you today in your heart. Recite them to your children and talk about them when you are at home and when you are away, when you lie down and when you rise" (Deuteronomy 6:5–7).

Placing leadership development at the center of organizing answers a key Christian directive: "The gifts Christ gave were that some would be apostles, some prophets, some evangelists, some pastors and teachers, to equip the saints for the work of ministry, for building up the body of Christ" (Ephesians 4:11–12). It upholds the First of the Seven Principles of Unitarian Universalism: The inherent worth and dignity of each person.

Practically speaking, developing leaders contributes to the long-term sustainability of a community organization. By investing in leaders and in their development, organizations gain the gratitude and commitment of those leaders for the long haul. By awakening in them a belief in their own capacity, and that of their peers, organizations build a strong leadership base upon which to achieve lasting success in their issue work.

This awakening of a belief in one's own capacity often begins with one's earliest interactions with a skilled organizer. And it's not always a pleasant experience, at least not at first. Mary Gonzales is a retired organizer and trainer who worked for the Gamaliel organizing network for twenty-eight years, from its inception. She describes an early encounter with the organizer who introduced her to the field:

> Greg said to me, "Why have you chosen to be poor, powerless and insignificant?" And I had a tantrum. I said, "That was God's choice, not mine." And he said, "Don't ever blame my God for the decisions you make!"
>
> That night I cried a lot. It was rage, and I had no clarity about it. I kept telling myself, "Something's gotta change, something's gotta change." And I didn't know what. I thought I was angry about that, that I couldn't figure it out. But later I realized it was that I couldn't believe I was so transparent to a stranger!
>
> But I remember this sense like I had to do something, because I was going to fall off the edge of the cliff. I had to do something, but I didn't know what. Then what happened was, it began with my dear, lovely mother, who would say, "Come on, I don't want to go alone." So, I'd walk along with her to the organizing meetings she was attending. And next thing you know, I'm involved in a campaign; and the next thing you know, I'm involved in another.

The realization that an organizer is as interested in a leader's development as any issue work can be a pivotal moment. I remember, early in my involvement in organizing, being invited to join a team of leaders that was going to ask a potential funder for a rather large contribution to our organizing work. At the team's pre-meeting, after agreeing on the format we would follow, the organizer turned to me and said, "Okay, what role do you want to take in this agenda?" Thinking that it would be best to play to my strengths, I said I'd be most comfortable leading the prayers at the beginning and end of the meeting. But my organizer looked me squarely in the eye and said, "Well, then, Pastor,

I think you should do something that you're *not* as comfortable with. How about you be the one who asks for the money?" I was shocked and a little terrified! I wondered why we would risk having me take on what I thought was the most important part of the meeting when I had never before played that kind of role. But my organizer was serious. And in that moment I realized that even asking for and securing money for our work was not as important as giving me as a leader a new challenge aimed at developing my capacity.

Other women describe similar moments of realization that their own development was paramount in the minds of their organizers. Stephanie Kolin was a young rabbi in Boston when she first learned this lesson:

> I got to be in a Greater Boston Interfaith Organization meeting with an independent candidate for governor. I was terrible in the meeting! I asked the dumbest questions! I had no idea what I was doing and I was way over my head. I left the meeting terribly embarrassed. We came outside after the meeting and I was apologizing and not sure what to say, and the organizer said, "Alright, let's talk about it. Go home first, though." (I was in tears at this point.)
>
> We talked about it later and I kept apologizing and trying to explain my behavior. And he said, "Listen: you weren't afraid to talk to power! You weren't afraid to come to the aid of your friend in the meeting when you thought she needed help. Just build on that. You have good instincts, even if you had no idea what you were talking about! We'll work on that. You did well in the room." I was like, "Oh?"
>
> Now, did I do well in the room? No. But the things he pointed out were things I could build on. He was great; a kind and compassionate teacher. He didn't write me off. And he saw me as a rabbi of an institution that he wanted to work with. I got that. It was good. He invested deeply in me, and it taught me.

Pamela Twiss was co-director of Minnesota's ISAIAH organization and now serves as the training director for People's Action. She told about one of the first big public meetings that she planned as a new organizer. It appeared that it would go very well, given the number of people that were expected to turn out for it, the involvement of key leaders, and the agenda they had planned.

But Twiss and her leaders hadn't counted on the fact that a small but vocal group of detractors had heard about their plan and organized a loud protest outside the doors of the church where they were meeting, which eventually spilled right into the meeting space. Because of the angry clash between the original leaders and the protesters, the meeting was called off just minutes into its start time. Here's how Twiss describes what happened in the aftermath:

> I almost gave up organizing then. It felt like it was the worst public meeting in the history of public meetings! I thought I'd be fired. But my organizer asked

me, "What did you learn?" I said, "That's your question?" That's the only thing he cared about; I couldn't believe it! It was awesome. He didn't care about the organization's reputation. He cared about what I learned.

Jeannie Appleman is a Jewish lay woman who is a recognized expert in training rabbis in the principles of organizing. She remembers what it was like to be mentored and shaped by a skilled organizer early in her exposure to the field. She makes reference to what's known in the organizing field as the Iron Rule: Never do for others what they can do for themselves:

> He used the Iron Rule with me in a way that was deeper and harder. He would just tell me that I was wrong! There was no sugar coating of anything! He knew me well enough—he bothered to know me well enough—that he knew how far he could push me. That work he did with me initially was really important, to ramp me up to a new level of capacity, and how I thought about myself. He was the first one to help me identify how organizing was changing me, especially regarding power; how engaging people and organizing around power was changing how I relate to power.

LEADERSHIP TRAINING

Because of this priority on developing leaders, one of the first things faith-based community organizing groups expect of those entering into this work is that they attend a leadership training event. Coming to terms with one's leadership capacity takes time and focused effort. So the training programs of all the faith-based community organizing networks are substantial in length (a week to ten days) and intense in nature. For one thing, there is a lot to teach about what organizing entails. But there also is a lot that each leader needs to examine, confront, and decide to change about herself in order to emerge from the experience ready and able to take on the issue challenges the organization intends to address.

Participants are told, early on in the training, that this is going to be as much about them as it is about the tools they will be trained to utilize. The "about them" part of their training is always the most difficult aspect of the experience. But it also can be the most liberating.

> Organizing training was like a door opening and a breeze coming in. It gave me a language, a methodology, a way to live, a way to think. It all made sense to me, like light bulbs going on in my head all ten days of the training, my head exploding the whole time! I come back and I'm like, "This is going to be my life's work!"

—Mary Gonzales

Power

The first thing these training programs call into question is our relationship with and attitude toward power. This can be particularly challenging for women, who often are socialized to view power as a negative force, or at least to shun power for ourselves. On day one, the trainers take us through a group role-play that reveals just how powerlessly we can behave when confronted by those who easily wield power over others. Then they challenge us to consider whether power is a positive, negative, or neutral force, and to discover what our sacred texts and religious traditions have to say about the matter.

One of the biggest "aha moments" for me at the weeklong training I attended was learning—from an organizer, not a pastor or biblical scholar—that the word power appears 324 times in the Christian Bible (NRSV). And power is lauded more often than humility, a term that appears only ten times! This revelation aroused downright anger within me, that I had not, in all my years of faithful church-going and seminary training, been made aware of this imbalance of emphasis. Instead, I had been led to believe that my highest calling was meekness and humility. No wonder I was so ambivalent about power, even to the point of rejecting its worth outright!

Power is a concept that comes around again and again in the field of organizing. It starts with challenging individual leaders to determine whether they want to be powerful or not, which is directly related to their ability to get anything of significance done in their lives and communities. Because that's what power boils down to: the capacity to do something; the ability to act. That's the basic dictionary definition of power. Given that, one can see why organizers lift it up as a positive thing, challenging leaders to come to more positive terms with it.

> Coming to an understanding about power has been important for me. And not being afraid of it, but that God gives power as a positive force. Power is going to exist, and if positive people don't take the power, negative people will. So I've come to a level of maturity where, if you are offered leadership constantly, you have to recognize that you're a leader and step into that. And also be willing to speak up when I see that things are wrong, in my organization or in the public arena. I'm more likely to speak up because I now believe that speaking up will help to create change.
>
> —Onleilove Alston

But the question remains: why do so many of us have a negative reaction to power? In part it's because we know the famous quote from the nineteenth century British historian Lord Acton: "Power tends to corrupt and absolute power corrupts absolutely" (Letter to Bishop Mandell Creighton, 1887).

Certainly we've seen that lived out in our lives and in our world. It's understandable, then, that we might shun power for ourselves; we're not interested in being corrupted.

> When I started getting exposed to organizing, I thought people were a little crazy because they kept talking about power! I had put that lens of corruption on power. But I've had a lot of evolution around that thinking. I used to be deferential to people who wanted to put me into leadership positions. I wasn't embracing power because all I could think of was that old model.
>
> —Onleilove Alston

When women consider our relationship to power, extra baggage comes with it. In many cultures and times, women have systematically been denied power. Furthermore, women have long been prime victims of power gone corrupt, in our private lives as well as in the public realm. Perhaps we fear wielding power in similarly destructive ways, or fear an abusive backlash if we start acting powerfully.

> I had had power used over me and my family, and I didn't want to do that. I didn't want *no* power, though. I didn't like powerlessness. But I didn't want to be an aggressor. That propelled me to think about what kind of power I did want, and to ask, "Why not me?" Why not go and take the power, like everyone else, and not worry that I would be corrupt, like I'd seen others become?
>
> —Louisa Fletcher-Pacheco

Fear of power's tendency to corrupt isn't all that makes us wary of claiming it. For with power comes responsibility; the greater the power, the greater the responsibility. Jesus said something similar, recorded in Luke's Gospel: "From everyone to whom much has been given, much will be required; and from the one to whom much has been entrusted, even more will be demanded" (12:48). When we wield power, we become responsible for actions that affect others. When we're not the ones in power, we can always blame someone else if something goes wrong. Power involves risk; and risk might lead to failure. And most of us prefer to avoid failure.

Additionally, people who exercise power must deal with tension, controversy, and outright conflict. So we might ask ourselves: do we really want (more of) this in our lives? Many of us were raised to avoid such unpleasantness. And we may not have learned the tools to manage it constructively.

> There are people who are your colleagues who think it's "taking over" when you exercise your power. But I think it's smart to exercise your

power. Having a healthy understanding of power allows you to take some risks. For women, community organizing can offer a pathway for understanding, appreciating, and practicing public power, which I think is really important. A woman can take this stuff into who she is and figure out how to have more agency, how you're going to negotiate who you are in public, and that you get to decide that for yourself.

—Karen Brau

For me, deciding to take risks and embrace power has meant fighting my habit of smiling every conflict away, my tendency to calm all the waters around me. I've had to learn to deal with people being angry around me, even at times angry *at* me. I've also learned, though, that risking controversy for the sake of my values wins me the respect of others. In fact, I have deeper relationships and stronger partnerships with people with whom I've worked through conflicts. I've learned the value of tension as a creative force, as an indicator that something truly important is stirring, that God's Spirit just might be blowing up a storm of positive change.

If we acknowledge that we as individual and communal believers are called to be powerful, it's important to remember the sources and context of our power. As people of faith, we believe that our only legitimate power comes from our relationship with God. We are children of a powerful Divinity, in whose image we are created, both male and female (Genesis 1:27). God gives us capacity and ability: "You shall receive power when the Holy Spirit comes upon you" (Acts 1:8).

If and when we do lay claim to our God-given power, the only way to fend off the temptation of corruption is to wield our power in the context of healthy human relationships. This in part is why, in faith-based community organizing, there is such a fundamental emphasis on building relationships. When we serve with others who also have chosen to wade into the risks of power and influence, we are more likely to be held (and to hold them) accountable.

Lutheran pastor and author Dennis Jacobsen writes in *Doing Justice: Congregations and Community Organizing*, "We need the community . . . because we are battling principalities, powers, and wickedness in high places. On our own we would be ineffectual, co-opted, or crushed. As a community, we experience a power that is greater than the sum of its parts. Within the community, we discover gifts, abilities, and power that we did not realize we had. As a community, we are emboldened and empowered to take stands and engage in struggles that we would not conceive of doing on our own" (70).

Earlier I referenced the well-known quote from Lord Acton about power's corruptible qualities. And I quoted from Jesus, whom I consider *my* Lord, about the power of the Holy Spirit bestowed upon God's people. It was a great gift to me, coming into the realm of community organizing, to learn of yet another person with a royal moniker, Audre Lorde, poet and 1980s human rights activist. Lorde knew first-hand that claiming and exercising power doesn't eliminate our fear; it simply trumps fear's power over us. Lorde said, "When I dare to be powerful, to use my strength in the service of my vision, then it becomes less and less important whether I am afraid" (*The Cancer Journals*, 17).

So then, in service to God's and our own vision for a more just society, faithful people claim, build, and use their power for good. We intentionally increase our ability to get things done.

Self-Interest

Faith-based organizing spoke more to me than the tenant and anti-intervention organizing I had done, which did not engage the whole person, either me as an organizer or the leaders. Before I was only organizing one slice of this person's life and interests. I wasn't figuring out who this whole person was. That whole concept of self-interest, direct and enhanced—self-preservation and self-realization—both are really how I think about organizing people now. I found over the years that as I have gotten more comfortable in my own skin, with my own story, and understanding the different ways it has impacted me and fueled my public life, it has completely enhanced my capacity to help others uncover why they're attracted to justice work.

—Jeannie Appleman

Another concept that community organizing training deconstructs and harnesses is that of self-interest. Culturally, the term holds negative connotations. I type it into my computer's thesaurus and it gives me the term selfishness as a synonym. I think about politicians who often are accused of acting only out of their own self-interests, implying that they don't take their constituents' or the broader community's needs into consideration.

At training we learn that self-interest, like power, is better understood as a positive and ever-present, though often subconscious, force. It is set in contrast to selfishness, on the one hand, and selflessness on the other. It is shown to be a much more relational term than either of the other two. Even the Latin origins of the word *interest* bear this out. It's a compound from *inter*, which means among, and *esse*, which means to be. So, the trainers insist, self-interest can best be understood as the self existing among others. Self-interest falls between the extremes of selfishness and selflessness and is a much healthier, relational, and more productive pursuit.

Why this shift in understanding matters so much in community organizing is because it's important to get people in touch with precisely why they care about issues of justice and equity. Why is it in your own self-interest to pursue a particular issue? What experience or value do you have that lets you identify with this concern? And what will you gain, directly or indirectly, if we foster change regarding it? Getting in touch with the what's-in-it-for-me? dynamic fosters honesty and leads to a deeper, more personal, and likely longer-term engagement on the part of the leader.

> In my first exposure to [secular] organizing, I was never asked about my own self-interest. You had to be covert about how to get it met. I just knew I should do things right and make people happy. I was in service mode. I completely burned out because I was disconnected from my own self-interest. I was in my default way of being, which is, "How can I help you?"
>
> But I was making nobody happy, especially me. I would work all the time and I just couldn't work hard enough to be worthy of anything. I was completely baffled. And nobody respected me, because you don't respect people who are obsequious like that. I never had an opinion! I never tried to direct things in any direction. I was selfless. People do not respect that!
>
> Understanding the whole self-interest, selfish, selfless continuum was the most important part of my first [faith-based] weeklong training. "You mean I can say out loud what I want to do?" That was amazing!
>
> —Pamela Twiss

People who claim to care about matters of justice primarily out of a desire to be selfless servants to those "in need" can either be too passive for their own and the organization's good, as Twiss experienced, or they can convey a certain self-righteousness that is demeaning to those they are hoping to help. Such an attitude, even if unconscious, gets in the way of seeing one's neighbor as a whole person, with assets as well as needs to bring to the table, as a potential partner in the establishment of greater justice. And, just as importantly, a focus on altruism alone can mask the actual but repressed neediness of the one who would rather be seen as the selfless helper.

This evolution toward embracing one's own self-interest can be an especially difficult journey for women. Rather than understanding and harnessing our own self-interests, women traditionally are encouraged to be selfless beings. Women of faith often have the added burden of religious traditions and scriptural interpretations that emphasize self-denial, even self-sacrifice. Operating primarily out of these impulses can wear one down and even generate resentment over time. Compassion fatigue and hard feelings don't nurture relationships and the gritty determination necessary for building the kind of power that creates long-term social change.

> I remember once as I was leading a training session on self-interest and telling how my disabled brother Bobby was always my motivation for the

early work I had done. And in that moment I realized that my own desire to be free was a big part of my motivation. But I hadn't ever wanted to admit that, because I thought I needed to do all of that out of selflessness and care for my brother and my mother. All of a sudden I realized that my own self-interest was a factor and it was legitimate to have one! But I had never allowed myself to think or say any of that until that moment.

—Mary Gonzales

Although I have learned to harness my own and the self-interests of others in my organizing work, I know that the term itself remains problematic for many people of faith. So I have found it helpful to equate it with the concept of vocation. For certain faith traditions, my own included, we even have a "doctrine of vocation" that has to do with all the ways God calls us to express our giftedness in the world. When I teach about exploring and embracing one's self-interest, I encourage people to think about it as "what God is up to" in, through, and surrounding their lives. Theologian Frederick Buechner has succinctly defined vocation this way: "The place that God calls you to is where your deep gladness and the world's deep hunger meet."[1] *That's* self-interest.

Acknowledging, even embracing one's own self-interest also finds theological affirmation in the biblical commandment "Love your neighbor as yourself" (Leviticus 19:18b). If I haven't learned to love and value myself—my own needs, gifts, and motivations—how will I know how to love and serve my neighbor? Too often we rush in and try to love our neighbor without fulfilling this *as yourself* prerequisite of the commandment. Getting clear about one's self-interest in an endeavor brings one's motives to the surface, making them easier to understand and build from. It fosters a directness of intent that helps others around you deal with you with greater clarity.

> After I went to weeklong training, I went home and decided I wanted to do this work for pay. The self-interest piece at training was important for me, to figure out what was motivating me. I said to my organizer, "If we're going to form a new organization in the western suburbs, I want to be doing this for pay by the end of this year." That's exactly what happened, less than a year later.
>
> —Maureen Geddes

NTOSAKE

The venue that most helped me get clear about many of these concepts I've been describing was the Gamaliel organization's unique three-day training

Chapter One

program for women, called Ntosake. The word is African in origin and means "She who walks with lions and carries her own things." Mary Gonzales and a few other prominent women in the organization conceived of it in 1996 in response to challenges by women that Gamaliel's weeklong National Leadership Training was too male-centric and did not acknowledge the unique gifts women bring or the roles they play. Ntosake was not designed to replace weeklong National Leadership Training, which all leaders are expected to attend. But it does provide an important supplement that can be transformative for women.

Mary Gruber from Minnesota was instrumental in shaping the Ntosake movement. Here's what she remembers:

> I was sick of the perception and the expectation that, as a woman, I'm only good for making coffee! We were ignoring the role of lay leaders and how women were treated differently than men. I was very angry, but I didn't have the right venue for expressing myself.
>
> I was one of two leaders (who were not organizing staff) who helped create Ntosake. We were helping women identify for themselves what their own demons and barriers were to being as powerful as they could be, even within their own organizations. It wasn't just about trying to get a meeting with the mayor. It was also about trying to deal with that pastor or organizer over there.
>
> It wasn't just me that was having these issues. It was many of us. I struggled with and pushed for what I wanted out of it. Even some of the celebratory aspects or rituals—the whole spiritual environment that we created, which was so important—I wanted built right into the training, not just as bookends.

What's so unique about Ntosake? At Ntosake training, women are separated from the real or perceived expectations of their male counterparts and are able to encourage and challenge one another out of their common female perspectives. More time can be devoted in training sessions to the unique ways that women struggle with concepts like power and self-interest; with the ways that women, more so than men, are raised to develop rich private realms to the neglect of influential public lives.

To a significant degree in these settings, women respond more positively to the affirmation and agitation of female trainers and peers because the undertones of male superiority or abuse are absent. And, removed from their male-dominated religious traditions, women are able to create authentic rituals that more deeply resonate with their sense of the Divine. Free to weep, shout, swear, dance, laugh, or sing without shame or fear of judgment or rebuke by men, women who attend Ntosake trainings emerge empowered and equipped to take on significant leadership roles in their congregations, organizations, and communities.

Here are some anonymous remarks I recorded at an informal gathering of Ntosake alumni who were asked to share what the training has meant to them:

You learn to silence the negative voices in your head and to say, "I am awesome!" My sisters help me with that. And that gives you the confidence to take on any issue.

I was fighting my own battles at home to not be the wife and mother 24/7. Ntosake helped me get my voice, got me out of the house and into the public arena.

I came back from the Ntosake training and felt I'd had a rebirth. [The trainer] helped me see that I was doing all this waiting on people but never got to claim any real leadership. She asked me why I couldn't get over being a babysitter and claim my power. Now I know I'm powerful, so I keep going back to Ntosake, which is like a Mecca to me!

Ntosake held up a mirror to things I was doing to undermine myself. I was always there for everyone else but wasn't putting myself in the equation.

There are things in us that are hidden and have to be brought into the light. Ntosake makes you do that in a way that's safe and challenging at the same time. So you're ready to change the world!

Ntosake forced me to move some of my work from my head to my heart and my guts. We learn to be okay with our dents and scratches and see them as medals.

I find it so energizing to be with amazing and inspiring women from every walk of life, ready to be transformed. I find there's still so much a male way of being in our organizing. Women need to find their voice and to stand in the midst of that.

I have demons of self-doubt, voices telling me, "You're not the one." At the Ntosake training, the façade that keeps me from taking greater risks and greater leadership in my life began to tear down.

When I had a chance to go to Ntosake, I so appreciated the focus on women, by women, and the focus on power. Now I want my granddaughter to go!

Ntosake? I loved it! The stuff about public/private meant a lot to me. Now, my family is struggling with my new passion for public work and a public life.

I always wanted to lead, but had never been trained or invited. My time at Ntosake was so enlightening and motivating and transforming. Some shackles were loosed and broken. The fear of feeling inadequate was taken over by feeling powerful! It brought something out of me so that I'm looking forward and I'm not going back.

Public and Private

Some of the women commenting about Ntosake alluded to the discovery and embracing of a public life. When engaging in community organizing, this is another concept that women often have to grapple with to a greater degree than men: the difference between their private and their public lives. Confusing the two, or acting as if our public relationships are ruled by the same principles as our private ones, can make it difficult for anyone to be effective in public leadership roles. Women more so than men are expected and trained to cultivate our private lives and relationships more fully than our public lives and relationships; so, distinguishing between the two or creating a healthy balance of each can be difficult. To be an effective and powerful actor in the public arena, one must gain clarity about the rules and expectations—mostly unwritten—that dictate how one behaves.

When my father died of a sudden heart attack at age 74, I saw up close what happens to too many women with regard to taking private relational habits into public relationships. My dad had always been the one who took care of all their financial matters. But because he died unexpectedly, neither my mom nor my siblings and I knew much at all about how he had kept track of those affairs.

Not long after my dad's death, my mom was introduced to a financial planner who worked in her retirement community. Mom met her at a cocktail party, one of many that this woman hosted in the homes of other retirees. Anxious about her own ignorance regarding her financial situation and lured in by the charm of this woman, Mom quickly accepted her offer to become her financial advisor.

As executor of her estate, at first I was relieved that Mom had some help in figuring out her finances. But when I finally was able to investigate more closely what was going on, it became clear to me that Mom needed to get out of this relationship. Her financial planner had taken too much control of Mom's finances and was making decisions that weren't in Mom's best interest. Mom understood the need for this move, agreeing that she wasn't being well-served financially. Still, it was extremely difficult for her to separate her feelings of friendship and loyalty to this woman from the practical realities of the situation.

But it was clear to me that this woman wasn't out to make a bunch of new best friends from among my mom and her peers. Rather, by hosting sociable gatherings for vulnerable retirees, she was cultivating their trust and thereby gaining their business. My mom, who was so good at nurturing private relationships, didn't get that applying those same relational habits in public could be detrimental to her long-term well-being and that of her heirs.

In community organizing, this blurred distinction between one's private and one's public relationships is sometimes referred to as "looking for love in all the wrong places." To help would-be leaders understand the importance of the differences, trainers draw a side-by-side chart of what should characterize our private versus our public lives.

Table 1.1. Public and Private Relationships

Private	Public
Seek affection and friendship	Seek respect and partnership
Casual, intimate	Formal, out in the open
Peace, harmony, accommodation	Tension, conflict, agitation
Gain love	Gain power
Just be yourself	Masks, uniforms, roles to play
Sacrifice, willingness to forgive	Accountability, consequences
Fluid boundaries	Strict boundaries
Lasting care or lasting resentment	No permanent friends or enemies

Embracing a public life can add depth and richness to a woman's existence. It can also compel her into relationships and arenas where decisions are being made that deeply impact her quality of life and that of her family and neighbors. It stretches her to learn new skills and uncover gifts she may not have known she had. Karen Brau, a Lutheran pastor in Washington, D.C., describes how becoming active in community organizing created a lifeline for her when she was facing a crisis in her private life:

> I had gone through a divorce not long before getting involved in organizing and that was really debilitating, personally. So to have a place to practice that was bigger than my home life and my congregation was part of my own reformation. Practicing being powerful and acting in a larger arena was really important.
>
> When you're divorced, it's always hard and it takes a long time to recover. I was able to have life-giving public engagement after all the struggles I'd had. I learned better public speaking, better how to talk to a room full of people, how to understand the parts of a public meeting where you have to pin someone and really be prepared within yourself, all of these really great lessons. And how to build a group of people around an effort. Those were all really life-giving to me.

For many women it's an experience of liberation simply to begin seeking meaning beyond the familiar ken of our private realms. But in the process, women also can experience a level of anger we've not known before. This can happen as we grasp how the intense focus on our private realms has allowed others, mainly White men, to hold the reins of public power, creating advantages for the few over the many.

Anger

> I was angry about a ton of things: about how my father had lived and contributed in this country and worked his ass off but was always treated as a second-class citizen. I was angry about my church, the racism that was happening in our parish against the Mexicans. I was trying to figure out what to do about my disabled brother, to get him the services he needed. I was angry about the fact that my kids couldn't play safely in the front yard, but I didn't think there was anything I could do about it.
>
> I was in a tremendous internal battle about my marriage, with my husband wanting me to quit going to church or to the organizing meetings, or he wanted me to stop working, but then he'd want me to work again. So I was in this angry, confused mess all the time.
>
> —Mary Gonzales

Anger can have a paralyzing or detrimental effect on us, especially if we don't know how to express or channel it well. Women especially often are socialized to repress and deny our anger, or to express it in ways that feel to us or appear to others more like sadness or fear. I know that's how I often experience and express my own anger, by feeling sad or afraid and starting to cry. What that does to me is produce a sense of shame, a feeling of being out of control or wanting to hide. For others around me that can prompt caretaking or the urge to view and treat me as weak or child-like. Those feelings of mine and behaviors of those around me do not empower me! Rather, they drive me back into submissive tendencies and keep others, especially men, in their own traditional, more powerful roles.

But anger can become fuel for seeking greater power and self-determination. With encouragement and agitation from peers and organizers, we can channel our anger toward effective action. We can turn what might feel like hot, untamed rage into something more useful: cold, hard determination. Organizers helped me understand that anger is not a bad thing in itself. Rather, anger is a natural signal that my values have been violated. It's something to pay attention to, to assign merit, not to mask, deny, or ignore.

> I started looking at my story from a larger narrative perspective. I started to see not just my brokenness, but my woundedness. I was learning not to just be a victim, but a powerful being as part of a larger collective.

It also created anger in me. I became aware of how the market makes money off of people suffering, like how women feel about themselves, which contributed to my own eating disorder.

I discovered that my wounds were not just my own, and that there was resurrective and transformative power in the sharing of those wounds. It was liberation. I was in a way healed and freed from that part of my story by claiming and owning it.

—Melissa Reed

Still, both my upbringing and my faith journey taught me different attitudes toward anger. For example, when my father would get angry, I often felt frightened and confused. Though he was never abusive, he was a large, imposing man. And he could be loud and commanding. But then he would often distance himself from the rest of us, perhaps as his own way of managing his anger non-aggressively. I feared both his initial volume and then his withdrawal, since I craved his approval and attention, which normally were generous and loving.

Then there was the Bible camp counselor I adored who one summer had us memorize this New Testament passage and meditate on it for the entire week: "Dearly beloved, let everyone be quick to listen, slow to speak, and slow to get angry; for anger does not make you good, as God intends you to be" (James 1:19–20, translation unknown). I did so want to be good, for God's sake! And I had other Bible passages rattling around in my pious head about anger as a bad thing. But I hadn't yet noticed that plenty of my revered biblical figures got angry. Granted, some used their unbridled anger at cross-purposes from God; but many used their righteous anger to fuel their work for God's justice. Witness Jesus who, out of righteous anger regarding proper reverence for God's house, forms a whip of cord and drives the merchants and money-changers out of the temple (John 2:13–17).

Organizing woke me up to the significance and value of my anger, and it gave me the insight and skill to harness it for my own and the greater good. One of my most influential organizing mentors has more than once helpfully pointed out to me that, when I am angry about something, and clear about the values being violated that trigger that anger, I am a much more effective trainer and organizer of others. When I'm lagging in spirit or imagination in this work, he has taught me to get back in touch with my anger, either about things from my past, or better yet, about things that are ticking me off right here, right now.

Organizers remind us that anger can outweigh fear. I had seen my mom work more than full-time and not make ends meet. I was very angry at that injustice. There was a fight and outrage in me. In order to direct it and have it be productive, that propelled me into the tenant organizing work I did in the Bronx. It propelled me to the doors and to do the work in a new space. I was so angry. But I was learning to politicize that anger and use it as fuel. That was huge.

—Louisa Fletcher-Pacheco

Mary Gruber was part of a select set of leaders who went to South Africa periodically to support the work of the Gamaliel affiliates there. On one of those trips, she led a delegation that met with the U.S. ambassador's staff, in an attempt to get U.S. funding to South Africa for treatment through the President's Emergency Plan for AIDS Relief, or PEPFAR program. In dealing with the situation, she found herself getting angry about how the delegation was being received. Here's how she channeled her anger:

When we went to the embassy, we had to meet with the concierge, a very arrogant guy. They ushered us into a room that was set up like a classroom. Clearly they were going to show us slides. And I just said to the concierge when we started our meeting—we had bishops Hanson and Olson and a bunch of South African church officials with us—I told him right from the get-go, "I see you were going to give us a presentation. But we've done our homework. We don't need a presentation on PEPFAR. We have an agenda and we would like to move forward with it, if you would be kind enough to listen. We didn't travel 3,000 miles to watch a slide show. We want to know what it will take for us to get this funding for these people." Eventually some funding did come through, but I don't remember all the details.

What Gruber *does* remember is how her anger clarified her vision and her role.

AGITATION

I had grown up playing sports and I'd had coaches that were like Bobby Knight. So none of the agitation at training shocked me. I always had figured out as a female how to operate in whatever competitive or confrontational paradigm was offered. I was never phased by it. I found it helpful in the reality that nothing around power is easy or un-messy, ever. So I knew that this was for real.

If you're going to travel in this way, you had better be clear who you are and what your power is and how you're going to have other people's backs and make sure that you're part of something so people have your back too. You can't do it alone. You're often times up against principalities and powers! I didn't see a gentler, kinder way to engage than the agitational model I saw at training.

—Karen Brau

In my introductory story for this book, I recalled my first encounter with Mary Gonzales as a trainer at a Gamaliel event for clergy. I described how she worked the space, using an aggressive Socratic method. She leaned in close to confront participants. I told how she "worked me over" for several minutes. And I recounted how I felt like I had never before been taken so seriously by someone who didn't know me. The encounter left me feeling, "convicted yet affirmed, challenged yet accepted, judged yet validated." I portrayed what Gonzales demonstrated as "the most effective relational tool for moving a person from where they are to where they need to be."

All of that is what we refer to as agitation, a key discipline in community organizing. Perhaps over most other things, because of the centrality of this practice, some people of faith have a negative view of organizing and choose not to engage in it. Given my own mild-mannered behavior in my early days as a pastor, one might think that the role of agitation in this field would have been enough to scare me away as well. But for some reason, that was not the case. For some reason, it was exactly what hooked me and propelled me to explore the field more fully. All I can imagine is that I was hungry to be taken that seriously, to have people dig deeper to find out what I cared about, and whether or not the ways I was behaving reflected the faith values that I claimed to hold. I also longed to have that kind of effect on others.

The various faith-based organizing networks employ the tool of agitation in different ways. Some place it front and center in their training programs and beyond. Others use it more in direct one-to-one encounters with the leaders they are developing. All of them, though, in varying degrees of intensity, demonstrate the importance of agitating public officials and others in positions of power in order to hold them accountable to the changes they are trying to make in the public arena.

> I had many small break-throughs in giving up the care-taking behavior. My supervisor told me I needed to agitate a certain pastor. I hadn't agitated any clergy yet. So I developed this whole agitation and I rehearsed it and I went and did it.
>
> Well, the pastor was pissed; and anger is not his leading emotion! But I pissed him off and I don't think I moved him. But my supervisor said, "Well that's good, you pissed off a pastor. Now you don't have to worry about that anymore. You survived." It got me past a hurdle. It was a victory!
>
> —Pamela Twiss

In the pursuit of leadership development within an organization, agitation is a powerful tool. And it's a tricky one. Because, when wielded ineffectively, it can drive a leader away or even cause harm. In the account Twiss describes above, her agitation didn't have the desired effect. But she also shared with me that the pastor she agitated did not walk away from organizing because of it. He had enough investment in the organization, and a strong enough relationship with Twiss, to stay in the struggle. Her story illustrates how agitation is really an art form that the serious organizer or leader must practice and hone in order to employ it well. I believe that it is one of the key things that makes organizing distinct from some of the other ways that people of faith engage one another and the public arena for the sake of doing justice. It is a tool for personal transformation that can develop leaders into powerful change agents themselves.

> Something I'm proud of as an organizer is that I've found that voice that helps me be a good trainer. It was organizers at Training of Trainers asking me what I wanted to become. Laura and Angela were in my face in intimidating ways, asking me if I wasn't worth declaring something about myself. Organizers agitate. It's what we do. I could feel that energy being invested in me. But I was also scared of it. That quest that Moses goes through resonates: "Am I the one? I don't think so!" Organizing has given me a quest to find out who I am and why I'm here.
>
> —Louisa Fletcher-Pacheco

The key to effective agitation has to do with tapping into the self-interest of the person you are agitating. Or, as Fletcher-Pacheco notes above, helping them find out who they are and why they're here. It's not about harassing them for disappointing you or the organization, although that might be one outcome of their behavior. Rather, it's pointing out to them how they have not lived up to their own best image of themselves through the behavior you observe.

Because agitation is based on self-interest, it's essential that you know something about theirs before you agitate them. That requires that you have enough of a relationship with them, or experience in their presence, to know what it is they want, what they value, who they hope to be in the world. When you observe them acting counter to those things, you have the right—some might say the responsibility—to point out to them what you see and hear.

There are plenty of biblical precedents for agitation. But most of us weren't taught to pay attention to those *as* agitation. Once I was exposed to the art of agitation, however, I couldn't read the Bible without noticing the frequency of such instances. A classic Old Testament example is where the prophet Nathan confronts King David regarding his treatment of Bathsheba and her husband Uriah (2 Samuel 12:1–14). In the New Testament, there's Jesus' post-Resurrection encounter with his disciple Peter, where he asks him three times whether he loves him, charging him a parallel three times to show that love by tending and feeding his sheep and lambs (John 21:15–17). The biblical reference that I most often quote when teaching about agitation is from the New Testament letter to the Hebrews:

> Let us hold fast to the confession of our hope without wavering, for the One who has promised is faithful. And let us consider how to provoke one another to love and good deeds. (10:23–24)

Provoking another to love and good deeds—to the doing of justice based on one's best abilities or aspirations—is the aim of an artful agitation.

There are essentially four steps to an agitation: (1) articulating the self-interest or values you believe the person holds related to this given situation; (2) identifying their behavior that you experience as contradictory to their self-interest or values; (3) helping them understand the consequences of their behavior for themselves and others around them; (4) getting a commitment from them to adjust their behavior to fit their values and self-interest.

Now perhaps that all sounds fairly benign. But the truth is, most of us have a hard time receiving agitation, even when it's as well-thought-out and delivered as the formula above prescribes. For most of us, a good agitation requires being jarred out of our habits or complacency. Someone might actually have to label our behavior in stark or what might feel like harsh terms before we understand the real consequences of how we come across.

In my own journey, a few labels have been difficult to hear but helpful to confront. "Do-gooder" is one; "people pleaser" is another; "nice girl" pains me to even type, though I used to wear it with pride! When organizers and other leaders have dared to call me out on such tame tendencies, I realize that I am not exercising the fullness of my God-given gifts nor participating powerfully in God's vision for a good and just world.

> When my husband came to pick me up at the end of training, I was like, "I don't know what happened to me this week, but whatever it is, this is what I'm going to spend the rest of my life doing." I loved every bit of it, the agitation, the way the trainers were. I didn't have any ambivalence.
>
> I remember Ana turning to some guy in the class who had said something to her, and she turned to him and just calm and cool she said, "it really makes me angry to hear you say that." It was just a direct and clear communication. She took no responsibility for his feelings. I thought that if I ever felt that much like a human being, that I would have lived a good life! That I could be that way with somebody, standing on my own two feet; it modeled something so you could see it.
>
> Training for me was people modeling how people could be human beings together: respectful, relational, mutually interested. That is how life is supposed to be!
>
> —Doran Schrantz

TRANSFORMED WOMEN
TRANSFORMING OTHERS

> Mike Gecan, my organizing mentor, told me to sit down and write a list of
> my five top leaders that I was going to think about, their whole life—what
> they're struggling with, what they're trying to move. He would ask "Are
> you going where they are or are you just expecting them to come to you?"
> He said he writes his names down and he puts them in his chest pocket. So
> now with my rabbis I tell them to put those names on their iPads or their
> phones and if they're not looking at that list frequently and cultivating
> those people, then they're not going to do it by themselves.
>
> —Jeannie Appleman

In this chapter I have focused on how women who participate in the field of
faith-based community organizing have been transformed by their engagement. I conclude this chapter by sharing some of the stories about how those
same women have seen themselves as agents of transformation in the lives of
other individual leaders.

Maureen Geddes was a key organizing mentor and colleague of mine during the years that I worked with ISAIAH of Minnesota. She recalls fondly this
opportunity to lead others toward greater self-realization:

> What I liked the best in organizing was working with people who said they
> could never do something. But through training and talking with them, I helped
> give them a voice. They learned these tools and could stand in front of people
> and work on things that they were interested in doing. They needed a vehicle,
> and our organizing gave them that.

Jay Schmitt, a fellow colleague of ours during those years, remembers this
about Geddes's impact on leaders:

> Her patience in terms of moving people was inspiring. She was not quick to
> write people off. That's a good lesson for all of us. She gave people time and
> kept working on them. She got stuff out of people that I'm not sure I would have
> thought possible.

Louisa Fletcher-Pacheco feels so strongly about the role she gets to play in
the transformation of leaders that she bothered to send me a follow-up text
message a couple days after I was with her face-to-face to interview her for
this book. Fletcher-Pacheco wrote:

> I wanted to loop back to that question you asked about my most proud moments
> in this work. It's been the people. And moments in the work where I have been

able to move leaders out of complacency and into power. Moments like in our Path to Power training when a woman from Able New Hampshire said to another participant who didn't like my agitational approach, "I need her to agitate me, to challenge me. Because when I go up against the snarl-toothed greed mongers who want to destroy disability rights, I can say, 'You ain't nothing! I've gone up against Louisa!'"

Sometimes the opportunity to open a door just a crack toward someone's transformation can happen in a simple one-to-one conversation. One might never again encounter this person. But if one takes a risk to meet them in a place where there is openness to new possibilities, it can have a profound effect. Mary Lim-Lampe, an organizer in Oakland, California, describes just such an encounter:

> I remember a one-to-one I had at my own weeklong training, with a woman who was only twenty-one. I remember asking her about her parents, whether they lived in the area. And she said, "My mom died when I was sixteen. But I never talk about that." I remember thinking, "Okay, so she's setting a boundary here."
>
> But I also thought, "Mary, you need to not leave her alone right now." There was something that told me that this was so shitty, what we're doing to this woman. So I asked her, "What is it like, not talking about it?" And her face changed and she was clearly relieved. And she said, "Oh, it's terrible! It's like I'm being asked to forget her all the time." And I said, "Well, what's that like?" And then she talked about her mom!
>
> I remember that so well. I realized the power of community then and the power of doing these one-to-ones and not leaving people alone. Our instinct is to leave people alone. But you need to have the guts to ask about *something*. Because we're not doing her a favor by not asking about it!

Karen Brau, a Lutheran pastor, connects the work she does in developing leaders to a very strong grounding in her own faith and calling:

> I feel most proud of developing leaders and having that be a fairly significant number of young people. They come here through various ways. Sometimes someone recommends that someone else coming into town look me up. Sometimes people discover that I'm pretty intense, and they wanted someone more easy-going! Some of that tendency comes from my training and experience in organizing. I'm direct and sometimes even demanding.
>
> I'm also pretty clear that I know I've been saved. I know God is for real. I think that causes me to have a level of personal fire that I come back to over and over. It gives me a confidence that, no matter what else is going on, I do have that.

Jeannie Appleman is a Jewish lay leader, with a different faith tradition and vocation than Brau's. But she also talks about how her faith comes into play as she participates in shaping leaders through this work:

> I actually believe more today than ever that the Almighty intervenes in human history on a regular basis. It's in the transformation of people that I see that. When I see a leader I'm working with allow organizing to transform them, I feel God's presence in that.

Tamisha Walker is a formerly incarcerated organizer who founded and directs Safe Return in Richmond, California. The leadership development and issue work that she does with her community of formerly incarcerated leaders has such far-reaching effects that she sees it reverberating out into the broader community where she lives and works:

> Organizing is transformational. I get to watch so many people who didn't know that they had the power to be informed, not just through research, but to do research that actually leads to change. They're taking action and building their own relationships, which can be the hardest thing.
>
> Formerly incarcerated people come through our organization to build power. We have people who have been through our training who went on to doctoral programs at U.C. Berkeley, after realizing, through this program, that they are valuable. We now have people who are working in the field of health care because that's what they were most passionate about. This helped them to identify those broader goals and their place in society. They'll always have the skills of organizing and they'll always be attached to Safe Return. No matter where they are, they'll be fighting for the liberation of other people.
>
> That's the transformational piece that I get to enjoy now, knowing that everybody that comes through Safe Return is not going to leave the same way that they came. It doesn't matter if it's one meeting, two meetings, a training. Whatever they're exposed to, they're not going to leave the same way. They'll have tools, a greater self-awareness, eyes opened.
>
> Some people come to our leadership training and the next thing you know you see them at a city council meeting advocating for something that they never would have before. You can be inspired by that! Okay, we planted a seed and something actually happened. That's the transformational piece for me.

Becoming a catalyst for transformation isn't necessarily a natural outgrowth of one's own transformation. Regardless of one's own developmental progress, it can be difficult to see the opportunities we have—some would say the responsibility—to intentionally work on developing others. Pamela Twiss, who over the years has had significant impact on my own and the lives of countless others, didn't always see herself in that role:

I came back from training knowing that my care-taking was a problem I needed to work on, dropping into pleasing leaders rather than agitating them. It took me a long time to see myself as someone who should be developing other people, who had opinions that I should impose and share. Unlearning all that was really a project. Staff colleagues were pushing me about the care-taker behavior all the time. And leaders were too. One of my leaders in particular was on me all the time about that. Leaders recognized that my taking care of them was not developing them!

Mary Gonzales shares her cheeky wisdom regarding what it takes to contribute to the transformation of others, with which I conclude this chapter:

We need to turn people's stories of victimization into stories of heroism, especially women. The heroine in a woman will defend anyone but the woman. The demon in a woman only focuses on the woman. How do we get the heroine to kick the shit out of the demon? I tell organizers they have to hug their leaders and tell them they're great, then you've got to kick them in the ass and agitate them. And then you've gotta go have a beer with them. You've gotta do it all.

NOTE

1. Frederich Buechner, *Wishful Thinking: A Seeker's ABC* (San Francisco: Harper-Collins, 1973), 119.

Chapter Two

The Transformation of Local Faith Communities

> When she and her household were baptized, she urged us, saying, "If you
> have judged me to be faithful to the Lord, come and stay at my home."
> And she prevailed upon us. (Acts 16:15)

LYDIA: PURVEYOR OF PURPLE GOODS AND CHRISTIAN COMMUNITY

In the Christian New Testament, in the sixteenth chapter of the Acts of the
Apostles, is the very brief account of a woman named Lydia. It begins when
the Apostle Paul and his traveling companions come into the city of Philippi,
where Lydia lives. On the Sabbath day, Paul and his friends go outside the city
gates to the river, because they have heard that it is a place where people gather
for prayer; a sort of open-air or "pop-up" synagogue. There they encounter a
number of women, whom they engage in conversation about Jesus.

Lydia is among these women and, according to the writer, "The Lord opened
her heart to listen eagerly to what was said by Paul" (16:14b). Whatever it is
that Paul tells Lydia, it has such an effect on her that she chooses to be baptized
into this newly emerging Christian faith. And not only Lydia herself, but her
entire household!

Eager to continue growing in her faith, Lydia invites Paul and his companions
to be her house guests during their stay in Philippi. Lydia's powers of persua-
sion also extend to others in town, as she begins that day to provide a safe place
for Christians to gather in her home. Paul and his companions return more than
once to stay with Lydia and to "encourage the brothers and sisters [gathered]
there" (16:40b).

Lydia's story is an early Christian example of how women, transformed by
their own insight and their encounters with wise mentors, foster transformation

among others who are on a shared journey of faith. Though the account about
Lydia in Acts is brief, scholars find enough evidence that hers was one of the
many homes throughout the region that Paul traveled where house churches
sprang up in response to the telling of the Jesus story. The heads of such
households were the de-facto pastors of these early churches. It appears that
Lydia, rather than any man, was the head of her rather substantial household,
sustained by the living she made selling expensive purple fabrics from the
region of Thyatira.

A NEW WAY OF BEING AND DOING

When the Apostle Paul and his companions were traveling throughout the
Middle East, spreading the story of Jesus, there were not yet many of what
could be defined as churches in existence. There were, of course, synagogues
where the Jewish people gathered for worship and as a faith community. But
more and more during this time, Jews who chose to follow the newly forming
Christian religion were being cast out of synagogues and shunned by other
Jews. By necessity, Jewish converts to Christianity were creating new models
and new venues to practice their faith.

There also were non-Jews who were drawn to a faith expression different from the prevailing practice of the Greeks and Romans, of recognizing
multiple gods. Such "worshipers of God," as they are sometimes described
in the Bible, did not gather in formal places of worship, but some of them
did form communities based on their faith. Lydia and the other women
whom Paul met at the river in Philippi were among this sort of religious
group, having met often enough there that the location was known as a
place of prayer.

The story about Lydia and her conversion serves as a biblical illustration
of how women have played pivotal roles in the transformation of local faith
communities. After Lydia heard the story of Jesus, and chose to be baptized
along with her entire household, she joined a growing movement of Christians who were shaping what it meant to congregate as a faith community—to
be the local church in her day. She and her companions went from being a
loosely connected prayer group meeting on the banks of the river to a recognized house church, attracting new Christians and providing hospitality and
shelter to traveling evangelists.

Many contemporary women who embrace faith-based community organizing contribute to significant changes that alter the nature of their local faith
communities. Several basic organizing attitudes and disciplines provide the
tools for such transformation.

CULTIVATING A RELATIONAL CULTURE

I was in seminary and my teaching parish was Resurrection in Oakland with Pastor Lucy Kolin. It was a powerful experience. They were, as a congregation, becoming engaged in PICO organizing. They were about to do an internal listening season. I got there in time for the training done by a local organizer.

It made immediate sense to me, that this was a way for the church to be the church. Like, you might talk about fellowship, but what does that mean? But people getting to know each other's stories and really getting to be with one another? That wouldn't happen if there wasn't a facilitated process.

—Melissa Reed

When congregations are first introduced to organizing, they often are encouraged to conduct a congregational listening season, sometimes called an "Inreach." It's a concentrated period of time designed to get people talking to one another one-on-one about their lives and about what matters most to them as people of faith. This process begins to build authentic relationships between people who, when they usually interact, tend to do so at more of a superficial level.

For an Inreach, a designated group of listeners is trained to host one-to-one conversations that build trust and intentionally invite their conversation partners to share on a deeper level. The listening process brings to the surface interests and concerns that people have about their own lives, their congregation, and the broader community. By raising these issues, and realizing that others share some of those same interests and concerns, people are more readily motivated to join together and do something about them.

Lydia Ferrante-Roseberry is a Unitarian Universalist minister in Boulder, Colorado. She describes a listening season in her congregation:

Within my first year as the new minister we introduced organizing to the social justice team. Our congregation did a series of one-to-ones internally and came up with access to healthcare for children as an issue lots of people were concerned about. But when it came to taking action, we had a hard time finding people in our congregation who were directly impacted.

In the area schools, there was a big gap between those who were eligible and those who were enrolled [in the Children's Health Insurance Program]. We tried to close that gap by increasing access to enrollment. But it didn't touch us at our core as a congregation. It was the newspaper headline that grabbed us, and solidarity organizing with people who were directly affected. There was something beautiful about it, but we were still doing it more for [other] people.

So we did another set of one-to-ones and the organizer came to me and said that they were noticing something and she wanted to make sure I was okay with bringing it forward. It was around mental health. They were noticing that there was real pain in the congregation about mental health. Now, I knew some of our older women had adult children with mental health issues that they never brought into the public part of congregational life.

I told the organizer I was ready to engage in that. It broke open something in the congregation that was so beautiful, to be able to be more transparent.

After conducting multiple one-to-one conversations, those who have served as the listeners come together to share the kinds of things they heard in their visits. This isn't about telling each other who said what about whom or who is dealing with what personal problems. Rather, it's about identifying themes, trends, and patterns from among the conversations that can indicate the current collective character, tendencies, and self-interests of the faith community.

Equipped with this fresh understanding, congregational leaders can choose from several paths forward. They can adjust their programing to more effectively meet the needs and aspirations of their members. They can invite new people into leadership positions based on their particular interests. They can take action on issues within and beyond their congregation that their members clearly care about. In each case, they can activate wider participation and ownership of the ministry because they have reliable evidence that members have a clear stake in engaging those matters.

SMALL GROUP GATHERINGS

Another way to foster relationships and deepen meaningful congregational life is through periodic gatherings of small groups. This isn't a new concept for faith communities, of course. But community organizing brings new methods and outcomes to an ages-old practice. Sometimes referred to as house meetings, these small group gatherings provide a venue to invite members, and perhaps neighbors and others, into a space where people talk and listen to each other about matters that interest or concern them.

Thoughtfully facilitated house meetings give people a chance to share their stories, hear those of others, and imagine creative ways to address issues of mutual concern collectively. By assigning a number of specific roles for the meeting—as hosts, stewards, facilitators, time-keepers, devotional leaders, and so on—people get to practice being in leadership roles, take ownership of what happens there, and develop a greater stake in what they want to see happen as a result.

House meetings are usually about uncovering particular issues and ideas that people have which a congregation might want to address, either internally or externally. But the model also can be adapted to take on a very devotional nature that deepens members' sense of connection to God, to one another, and their corporate call into the world. Maureen Geddes, a retired Catholic lay woman who worked as an organizer with ISAIAH of Minnesota for many years, describes how she adapted the house meeting model:

> The whole concept of house meetings that I learned about from a Catholic Sister who worked for the Industrial Areas Foundation in Texas was very intriguing for me. I wanted to put that together with Bible study and the ways that people were willing to come together for a concentrated Lenten discipline. So I came up with the idea of Living Lent, where we got various clergy from our organization to contribute sessions for each week.
>
> It was an ecumenical tool that worked for the [Christian] traditions that use the Common Lectionary and for those that don't. It was a way to get our organization's principles into a broader constituency in the member congregations. And it gave pastors that weren't involved yet something to use that didn't cost them anything but gave them a taste of our work.

I was part of the Living Lent process that Geddes describes. I was a parish pastor at the time and I had a relatively small group of congregational leaders working with me around our community organizing activities. Up to this point, we had struggled to garner involvement from more members of our congregation. We didn't want to be just a fringe group that did "that justice stuff" on the margins of the rest of congregational life. But we hadn't found the right approach to bring greater numbers into our work. When Living Lent came along, here was a new tool to try.

My core group of leaders and I identified and invited twelve people to be trained as Living Lent Bible study facilitators. Then we and those leaders started to recruit others—through direct invitation, announcements in church, and newsletter articles—to join one of the small groups that would meet throughout the season of Lent, at a variety of meeting times and locations. And it worked! We had approximately 75 people engaged in weekly Bible study, using a resource that emphasized the call of God to actively live out our faith values in the public arena.

What was different about Living Lent from conventional Bible study was the nature and depth of the discussion. A set of provocative questions prompted people to look for the communal rather than simply the personal implications of each Bible lesson. And the questions encouraged participants to consider concrete action steps that they could take both individually and collectively to live out the implied or explicit call from the lesson. As a result, people who participated gained new and authentic relationships and went beyond a purely devotional benefit from Bible study to action-oriented and corporate responses.

A TEAM OF LEADERS

I believe that every congregation in America should have a justice ministry [team]. I believe in it! (I believe that choir is still important, don't get me wrong. That's how I first got excited about the church I joined as an adult.) Now, I don't think it's DART's job to get every congregation in America. But in whatever city we're in, it is our responsibility!

I believe that what God has ordained for his people is that we should be working for justice. Because in that work, relationships get built and so does a better understanding of the community. There's a spirit of community that gets built, hurts that get healed, stereotypes that get broken down. I believe that this is such a great pathway for living out the word of God.

—Leah Wiley

When congregations first begin working with a community organizing group, most form a team of leaders that coordinates the process. Sometimes called the Justice Ministry, the Core Team, or the Local Organizing Committee, this group operates differently from typical committees or task forces that congregations are used to. Its membership is made up of people who someone, often a member of the clergy, has invited, out of a sense that participating on the team will not just fill out the team's roster, but will significantly meet that person's self-interest and utilize their strong or developing set of gifts and skills. Further, ideally each team member either already has a significant set of relationships with others in the congregation, or has the capacity for developing them, given some tools and strategies. So, whether or not each team member considers her- or himself a leader per se, they are that indeed; for they already or soon will have what could be considered followers. The cultivation of that base of relationships will come into play often throughout the course of the team's activities.

Prior to learning about organizing, I had not always made use of teams of lay leaders to get things done. More often I had chosen to depend on my own or my staff colleagues' expertise and energy. I fell into the trap of believing it would be more work to explain what needed to happen and get buy-in from others than it was to just do it myself. The development of my first Core Team in the congregation where I served as pastor helped me tap into one of the most effective ways of getting things done in the church and in the world that I have ever employed. This simple tool has been so significant for me that an oft-repeated and shared mantra of mine is, "When in doubt, form a team!"

I already had an idea of who I wanted on my first Core Team before we conducted our congregational listening season. But that was a very small group of people with whom I had formed an early affiliation. To fill out the Core Team, I invited specific people who I or others had identified in one-to-one conversations during our Inreach: people who expressed a particular concern about issues in our neighborhood or larger community; people who were frustrated with an unjust status quo, but lacked the tools and the vehicle for fostering change.

A few things were givens when our Core Team met for the first time. We would meet monthly. We would be the "connective tissue" between our congregation and our community organizing affiliate. We would cultivate and demonstrate the attitudes and principles we were coming to understand as part of an organizing culture, including: discipline, accountability, relationality, mutual investment, action-orientation, taking risks, thinking systemically, behaving powerfully.

Not everything was a given, though. No one dictated to us what issues we would take up. Instead, that would depend on the self-interests of our team members and on what we would hear were the self-interests of other members of our congregation and our surrounding community. Not yet a given was how our new team would function within the traditional structures of the congregation. We needed to build a relationship with the church council and an esteemed status with those leaders and other key stake-holders in the congregation. Initially and then annually we needed to make a case for the substantial dues that the congregation was expected to pay to be a member of our local community organizing group. All of these and other ways of being influential and effective as a team we had to experiment with and grow into over time.

Meetings

> Running effective meetings is like participating in a liturgical tradition, which is one of the things I cherish about my own Catholic faith. Those patterns can be transformational, instructing us as to how we should live out our faith in the world.
>
> —Maureen Geddes

One way that the Core Team functions differently than many typical groups in a congregation is the commitment to running effective meetings. When I do training sessions on this concept, it's always fun to start out by asking people to describe some of the meetings they go to in their congregations or other settings. It's apparently a very common experience to sit through boring, undirected, seemingly endless, purposeless meetings! By coming up with the list of things that happen at ineffective meetings, it's then easy to name the corollary opposite characteristics for an effective meeting. It's clear that people don't enjoy ineffective meetings, especially when they happen over and over again. But it's also clear that most people don't know what to do about this problem, especially when they are not the designated chair or convener of the meeting.

When setting up a new Core Team, having an organizer do a brief training on running effective meetings can be energizing and instructive. Besides drawing from people's past experiences of what it's like to participate in effective and ineffective meetings, it's a chance to challenge people about taking responsibility for what happens at meetings, regardless of the official role they might be assigned. When I suggest to people that it's their own fault when meetings don't run effectively, there's real tension in the room about that; they get defensive, even agitated! But by pointing out that they can actually change the dynamics by speaking up or acting differently, a new awareness and sense of agency often dawns on people.

This new approach to running truly effective meetings is often experienced as refreshing, even revolutionary! And it turns out it's not rocket science. What it takes is disciplined adherence to a set of mutually-agreed-upon commitments from those participating. Those commitments include: (1) that our meetings will be designed to take us into action; (2) that we will share responsibility for carrying out—*between* meetings—the decisions made *at* our meetings; (3) that we will hold one another accountable for the commitments we make. Additionally, we agree that our meetings will no longer be the time and space for: (a) protracted debates on a large array of matters; (b) extended relational interactions; (c) lengthy verbal reports. But because deliberating on topics, interacting relationally, and getting reports are all important, we agree that team leaders will come to our meetings with a *limited* number of proposals for us to consider. We agree that we will build in a *brief* time-specific agenda item for deepening our relationships, but commit to doing the bulk of our relational work between meetings. And we agree that reports will come to us ahead of time in *written form*, with time for highlights and clarifications, only, at our meetings.

Once these principles are agreed to, a general framework or template for meetings is followed every time the team meets. That template looks like this:

• Meeting at a regular day and time each period (monthly, every other month, quarterly, etc.)

- People holding themselves and their peers accountable to attend meetings regularly
- Meetings lasting between one hour, 90 minutes, or two hours, max
- Meeting agendas that are prepared and provided to members in advance
- Roles that are shared by multiple members and agreed to ahead of time (i.e., chair, minute-taker, prayer, discussion facilitator, time-keeper, evaluator, etc.)
- Prayer and theological reflection that are given appropriate attention
- Agenda items that have specific time allotments
- Time on the agenda to check on previous commitments and make new assignments
- Tension that is not squelched but expected, as it signals that something real is at stake
- Evaluation as a regular discipline at the end of meetings
- Meetings that start, stay, and end on time

It's amazing how willing people are to come to meetings that are run following these principles! "Meeting" is no longer a dirty word, but rather an essential tool for getting important things done.

DEVELOPING LEADERS

In chapter 1 I discussed the high priority of organizers to invest in and develop leaders. When congregations get involved in this work, that priority continues, with clergy and other key leaders essentially taking on the role of organizer in their own settings. When asked what is one of the most difficult aspects of leading in a faith community, clergy regularly respond that it's about sustaining and widening the pool of leaders who share with the professional staff the responsibility of leading the congregation effectively. How many times have you heard or uttered the complaint that we have the same small set of people doing the same things in a congregation, often ineffectively, for years? With an emphasis on identifying and developing leaders, organizing can be a real blessing, even sometimes a turning point, for the life of the congregation.

> While I was at Temple Israel in Boston, I tried to create spaces where leaders had agency. I did a lot of leadership development—with some of the best leaders I've ever gotten to work with. We have this tradition of the Ark of the Covenant that is carried in the wilderness. The way it's built is by everybody contributing as their heart so moves them. They give what they have. That's a theology that makes a lot of sense to me.

So I consider it my job to help people find what the gift is that they have
to bring to the moment. Because the ark can't be lifted alone. Everyone
hoists it to put it on multiple shoulders. That's what sacred community
looks like: hoisting that thing on their shoulders and then pointing in the
direction that's different than the place we are in now.

I found that the most important way I could spend my time was helping
my leaders get in the path of interesting experiences and then debriefing
with them after. It's how I was taught: my mentors and my organizers putting me in the path of meaningful experiences.

—Stephanie Kolin

Too often in congregations we recruit people into leadership positions simply
out of a traditional or organizational need to fill that position. With that as
our motivation, we might cast about for any warm body. We might approach
several people before someone finally relents—often out of a sense of guilt
or obligation. Once we've filled the position, we often walk away from that
leader, hoping or assuming that he or she knows or will figure out how to
fulfill the role. If we're lucky, the task we had in mind will get accomplished.
Still relying on luck, the person we recruited might stay in the position long
enough to further the work of that committee or task.

But when we take that approach, likely little else will happen. And the next
time we have a role to fill, we'll cast about again for who it will be this time
that we can talk into taking it on.

I invest deeply in my leaders. I will get their back anytime, all the time.
That's what builds effective teams. I've also learned not to be afraid to
point out problems and to speak honestly. I don't say, "You really mucked
that up!" I'm not saying, "How could you do that?" What I'm saying is,
"Hey, you made a call. I'm glad you made a call. Let's talk about that,
because that could have gone a different way. What if you had come at it
like this?"

The trust that I have with my leaders is deep because I really care about
them, I care about their life, I care about their self-interest, I care about
who they want to become in the world. If they want to try something new,
even if they're not going to be polished or perfect, I will prioritize that,
because the next meeting they're going to be outstanding.

The risk is often worth it. No matter how high-stakes the meeting might
be, let's do some learning, so that we can all get better at what we're doing.

—Stephanie Kolin

When we decide to invest in and develop leaders, while at the same time
meeting a need or filling a role, so much more can be accomplished. We

start by taking the time to get to know our members and to understand what it is that motivates, concerns, or might excite them; what's their self-interest? Then we invite them into roles that we believe will fulfill a particular self-interest of theirs, as well as meet an organizational need. We don't guilt them into taking on roles, or appeal to their sense of obligation. Rather, we point out to them why we have asked them, in particular, and what we think they as well as the congregation will gain out of their leadership. Then, instead of walking away from them once they've accepted the invitation, we stick with them, providing them with the training, coaching, agitation, and resources they need to be effective and successful in their role. We demonstrate that we value them for who they are and for who they are becoming, and in the process we deepen both our relationship with them and their commitment to the life of the congregation.

> For one woman, over the course of years, there was this continual challenge that I would pose for her: to come out from behind the coffee pot into greater and greater leadership roles over time, little pieces at a time. I showed care for the other parts of her life enough that she didn't feel used.
>
> That's one of the gifts of women in organizing is that we've taken the relational part to heart, which feels like a stereotypical feminine way of being.
>
> I watched her begin to have a clearer sense of her own worth. And that's a theological value for me, for the UU principle: the inherent worth and dignity of all people.
>
> Process theology has always attracted me in understanding God as the force of Love moving in the world, luring us into our highest potentiality. That feels like a big part of what organizing is.
>
> —Lydia Ferrante-Roseberry

I started to notice an interesting dynamic as I was investing in and developing leaders who served on my congregational Core Team. My pastoral colleagues began to ask me who, from this relatively new or previously untapped pool of leaders, I might recommend to serve on the church council or in other high-level leadership positions. They were aware of the changes happening in people and recognized their potential for greater leadership. I sometimes had to tell my colleagues to back off, at least for awhile, and not try to poach these leaders away from what it was that we were doing as a Core Team! But at the same time, I was thrilled that my efforts were proving fruitful, so that the value these leaders were bringing and would continue to bring to the congregation were being noticed and appreciated in wider circles.

Eventually, some of my Core Team leaders did take on other leadership roles, as council members and even congregational presidents. Their ability to be effective in those roles was directly traceable to the initial work I did in developing and investing in them. And, the disciplines, principles, and relationships we developed in our Core Team work carried over in the ways that they led and invested in others in their higher-level positions.

SHIFTING THE NATURE OF
A LOCAL FAITH COMMUNITY

I thought if I went and read Catholic Social Teaching or the UUA Seven Principles or the ELCA's mission statement, that's what I would find being followed out in those churches. I'm a very literal, visual person. If I saw people acting differently, I thought they were very weird Lutherans or wondered what kind of Catholics or UUs they were!

—Ana Garcia-Ashley

There is a good deal of lore and dark humor around the improbability of congregations embracing any kind of real change in how they operate. There's the one about how many congregants it takes to change a light bulb; the panicky answer being, "Change? Who said anything about change?!" Or in Christian circles, during Holy Week, when we recall the Seven Last Words of Jesus, we sometimes ask, "What are the Seven Last Words of the Church?" Answer: "We have always done it this way!" Truth is, it's hard to instigate change, even when we know that change is the only way we will remain faithful or sustainable as a congregation.

Who Is My Pew Mate?

For some local faith communities, the need to change arises from the kinds of people who are beginning to occupy the seats in the sanctuary. Emily Eastwood was a member of a Lutheran congregation in St. Paul, Minnesota that was experiencing the influx of a number of lesbian, gay, bisexual, and transgender (LGBT) people into their midst. The congregation had been involved for many years in the movement across the denomination to welcome LGBT people into their churches. But in 1990 their national faith body, the Evangelical Lutheran Church in America, was dealing with two congregations in California that had broken denominational rules by ordaining two lesbians and a gay man as pastors. Eastwood's congregational leaders decided to take a vote of solidarity with the California churches, as well as indicate their own willingness to call an LGBT pastor. But an unexpected number of church members came out of the proverbial woodwork to vote against these two motions. It had such a polarizing effect on the congregation that they started to lose members. Eastwood describes the process she was a part of following these events:

> After the polarizing votes, we went to some workshops on how to do one-to-ones. Then we purposefully matched people in one-to-one visits, aimed at developing a new visionary statement that looked into the future, to the year 2000, and what we wanted to look like as a congregation.
>
> What happened was that we matched LGBT people who weren't feeling safe after that polarizing vote with people who had expressed upset that we were even there with them in church. Why didn't we just go found our own church rather than taking over theirs, was the sentiment. The purposeful matching up of LGBT people or allies with people who were known to be opposed created an opportunity for relationship building.
>
> When we got to the development of our visionary statement, the vote was overwhelmingly positive that we would have a gay or lesbian pastor serving by the year 2000. Some of the people who had previously voted against the support of the ordinations actually changed their minds!

Who Is My Neighbor?

Another kind of shift can occur using the principles of organizing. A congregation can be changed from an entity that exists entirely for the sake of its members into one that is focused on its broader community of context. The starting point for this move is, once again, about building relationships. In fact, the one-to-one conversation that characterizes a congregational Inreach, as Eastwood described above, is the very tool for moving out into our neighborhoods and getting to know those living and working around us.

Melissa Reed is the pastor at Salt and Light (formerly Redeemer) Lutheran Church in Portland Oregon. She was called to help the congregation shift from being an aging, declining-in-numbers, inwardly-focused church to one that was growing and that better reflected and responded to the diverse demographics and concerns of its neighbors. Trained while at seminary in community organizing, Reed describes how she approached her work early in her call:

> The first year I did a lot of listening. I had tons of one-to-ones out in the community and internally. What I realized was that those two worlds were not just magically going to come together. Young folks were not just going to come in with new ideas and ways to revitalize an older congregation. Systems uphold their power. I didn't move a lot of change that first year, other than building relationships and getting clear that the church couldn't just transform on its own. Something more radical was going to have to happen.

Organizing was everything during that time. We created a team that was half congregation members, half not, for the initial neighborhood listening campaign. The questions were, "What are the pressures on you and your loved ones?" and, "What would a relevant spiritual community be like for you?" We invited people to reflect on the idea that relevant spiritual community would actually have something to do with their real lives and stories, with the things they were actually struggling with.

That was the first of many external listening processes that Reed's congregation conducted over a period of ten years. That initial process began to shape the different kind of organization that eventually developed, one that has a new Lutheran worshiping community, Salt and Light, at its heart, with a more broadly defined non-profit organization, Leaven Community, which surrounds it. Salt and Light and Leaven Community members now understand that a vital role they can play in their neighborhood has to do with how they utilize their space. Reed explains:

We come into relationship with people inside or outside through our listening seasons. Relationships bring people together creatively so that we can respond to what we're hearing. The use of the building came out of listening in the community and hearing from organizations that there's not a lot of space that's affordable. And that, for people of color, there's not a lot of space that's not completely dominated by Whiteness.

So now, some of the groups we have sharing our space are the Center for Diversity and the Environment; Cascadia Wild, which organizes getting people into nature for tracking kinds of experiences; the Northeast Portland Tool Library. We have a room that is the Living Intentionally in Our Neighborhood space (LION) that we've kept as an office for newly forming organizations of color. So it's an incubator kind of space. There's the African-American Breast-Feeding Coalition. There's a midwifery group of women and doulas of color. There's the Native American Coalition for breast-feeding. And we have our soap-making co-op.

Some of the space we give away for free, but we need to stop subsidizing everything. We need to be strategic about what we subsidize so that we can be sustainable. We have a goal of raising another $25,000 from our building in the next year, by being more strategic about the levels of rates we have and based on organizations' ability and how they fit into the shared mission of Leaven Community.

Building a Public Life for the Congregation

Being a community with one foot in the church and one in the wider community is essential. The church is never separate from the world. In fact, the people in the church are themselves in the world. So we have to not have a false dichotomy. Our relationships and spirituality need to be fueling our action, and our relationships and spirituality are rooted in action. Action is just really good liturgy, for me. So the world comes into worship and we take worship out into the world.

—Melissa Reed

Getting involved in community organizing definitely provides ways for deepening and sustaining congregational life and interests internally. But perhaps the greatest advantage is drawing the congregation out beyond its proverbial four walls and into its community of context in ways that are life-giving both for the congregation and for the broader community.

> When I got there, we had about 120 church members and many of them realized that a relationship with the neighborhood was something they wanted. They had lost that, and they wanted it back. So we started doing one-to-ones with members and within the neighborhood.
> Eventually we ended up building a skate park in one of the neighborhood parks. We worked with the city to build that, along with restrooms. And we worked on after-school programs. Working with youth in our neighborhood was a big connector across generations and across class.

—Lydia Ferrante-Roseberry

In chapter 1 I discussed the importance of individual leaders differentiating between their private and their public realms, and the value and process of constructing a rich public life. Congregations face a similar challenge if their entire identity is based on their worship life and the spiritual needs of their own members, with perhaps modest forays into their communities in the form of charitable work. But broadening the definition of what it means to be the faith community as one that exists both for us *and* for the sake of greater justice (not charity alone) in the world around us becomes possible and exciting with the tools of organizing. Karen Brau, pastor of Luther Place Memorial Lutheran Church in Washington, D.C. describes this process in her ministry setting:

> When I came to the congregation, there was really no reaching out to the immediate community happening. There was social ministry happening, but not neighborhood or relationally focused. That has come about in the last 5–6 years, through listening.
> That's why we now have a day camp ministry in the summer, with Latino families in the neighborhood. We also use our place as a teaching tool and with an understanding, theologically, that there are churches that see living out the gospel in a certain way, around justice; that it's not an aberration or apostasy.

Young adults and youth from all over the country come here to stay at our hostel and engage with our on-site Steinbrook Center for an immersion experience on gentrification and racial equity.

Helping to understand that your place and your liturgy are connected also is something I've brought. I took backyard gardening and put it in public, with our neighborhood gardens. I took liturgy and put it in public. To me, these are really important ways to witness. We use things like outdoor processions to be out and around and in the neighborhood.

We did that here recently, when it was time to put our Black Lives Matter sign out on the lawn. We blessed the sign during the main service indoors. But then at the end of the service we did a recessional and a ritual outside when we planted the sign in the ground.

Building Collective Power

As strong as some congregations are in terms of their spirit of community, even the best of them generally have their members dispersing individually out into their separate worlds and vocations after their weekly services conclude. True, members might feel that they've received from worship and the faith community essential spiritual fuel for the various challenges that they encounter in their daily lives. Many might be involved politically or active in social causes where their faith plays a role. But congregations also have the potential for carrying their strong sense of communal cohesion into powerful public arena engagement.

Early in my work as an organizer, part of my charge was to identify and recruit those Lutheran congregations in the ELCA's Minneapolis Area Synod that might be ripe prospects for joining the ISAIAH organization. I knew many of the area pastors, since I had served in two of our synod's congregations over a sixteen-year period. From my past interactions with pastors and lay leaders, I had some reliable observations and intuition about the character of certain congregations.

I remember approaching the co-pastors who I knew well at one of those Lutheran congregations. That church's reputation was that many—perhaps even the majority—of its members were active in the public arena as individuals who gave their time and talents to a myriad of social and political causes. The pastors were both dynamic preachers and fine theologians, each known for their own inclination toward the doing of justice. So the hook I used to draft them and their church into my quest for new ISAIAH members was what I presented as their growing edge: the opportunity to move out into the broader community as a collective—not just as individuals—to make a more powerful impact on the kinds of issues that they and their members cared so much about. I believe that authentic pitch is what convinced them to join our organization.

While serving as a rabbi at Temple Israel in Boston, Stephanie Kolin introduced the opportunity for members of her congregation to extend themselves—collectively—beyond their usual way of operating as a faith community. She describes in detail how she and a wise colleague pulled this off:

Question One was an attempt to get a ballot initiative that would ban the Massachusetts state income tax. It would have undone the funding for everything we cared about, for seniors, for kids with special needs, for roads, for things people need! I negotiated, with the help of my senior rabbi and our board, that I would preach my Rosh Hashanah sermon in a way that would let us put cards on the chairs.

About 4,000 people come through our doors on that high holiday. Everybody had a chance to sign a card that said (1) I commit to voting "no" on Question One, (2) This is really important to me, I want to get more involved, and (3) I disagree with this campaign; I want to talk to somebody.

That was the right move, to give people a chance to say, "I don't think this is a good idea or I don't agree with the way we're doing it;" things that would assure that this would still be their sacred home even if we were doing an action that they might oppose.

About five people turned in cards saying they disagreed. These aren't our opponents! They are members of our community and being in relationship with them matters. Most often we share a set of values and we just get there differently. Even when we don't share the same values, we share a sacred home. We're going to do funerals and weddings and prayer together, we're going to raise our kids together. So we need to stay in a relationship in a sacred and respectful way.

So I preached a sermon about the ancient Jewish code that we're not allowed to pray in a room that doesn't have windows. There's a lot of reasoning in the text behind that. I talked about it as: our prayer is supposed to draw us out, it's supposed to do something to us, to change us. What happens on the inside of our prayer spaces is supposed to affect how we are on the outside of those spaces. I raised the question about what it means to do politics in the sanctuary. And can the public square also take place there and are they maybe one and the same?

I didn't mention Question One. My senior rabbi came up in the announcement part of the service and said, "We are exploring together what it means to have the public square and the sanctuary be connected. Here's an opportunity to do that. On your seats you'll find this card." It was such a powerful moment. I learned a lot in that moment, including how not to be alone in what I was doing there.

Greater Boston Interfaith Organization turned out thousands of signatures, including those from our congregation, that would defeat Question One so that it didn't get on the ballot.

Joining Forces

> The knitting together of people and other community entities facilitates a
> kind of power that wouldn't otherwise be available. This is a way for small
> faith communities to have power in the public discourse, for the values of
> the church to be lived out publicly and make real change.
>
> —Melissa Reed

As congregations expand in their corporate identity, they're likely to build
more relationships with their neighbors and others around them. They gain
new institutional partners to help them grow in their ability to do faithful
and effective justice ministry. The best faith-based organizing happens when
people from a variety of faith traditions collaborate and when they join with
other non-faith organizations with complementary values and visions. Louisa
Fletcher-Pacheco started out as a tenant organizer before she discovered
faith-based organizing, almost by accident:

> I had been doing organizing among tenants in these apartments. But I had a
> hard time turning out a lot of people to public meetings. It was such hard work
> to get any turnout!
>
> But when the city wanted to move a filtration plant onto Fordham Rd. in the
> same community as St. Nicholas church, I started talking to the pastor about
> what that meant to him, and to the middle-class housing organization in the
> neighborhood. And suddenly I had 600 people instead of 40, like before! They
> saw their self-interest being threatened. And the pastor was preaching about
> it and talking with his community and saying we need to stop this thing from
> happening.
>
> So my organizing brain was really lit up, that we had to connect the institu-
> tions and churches in the area with the ordinary citizens and tenants, and align
> all their self-interests. That's how we stopped the filtration plant from coming
> into that neighborhood!

Connecting and collaborating with other congregations and organizations
makes it possible to have a greater impact in our communities than we can as
individuals or single congregations. And it puts the powers-that-be on notice
that we are a force to be reckoned with. Karen Brau tells what that was like
in the neighborhood where she was a pastor in Baltimore:

> We started doing stuff after the congregational consolidation had happened and
> we had settled in one place, in a building that had some abandoned houses right
> behind it and what would become vacant lots. I remembered, from the organiz-
> ing I'd been exposed to, to do a listening campaign; not to presume what to do
> with any of the space, but to listen in the neighborhood. I started doing that.

Then the local organizer who was working with a national network to begin something in Baltimore came to me and said, "You seem to be doing what we're doing, only on a small scale. Would you consider being a part of this?" The organization hadn't been named or formed yet. It was just in the process of starting, with a small coalition.

For me, I realized that all the challenges of my neighborhood didn't happen in a vacuum, just because everyone there is falling apart. There were bigger forces at work. I could apply as many band aids as possible and create new things and still, what existed was always bigger than the place. I knew that, and that's what made me want to get connected with something else.

I understood structures and it didn't make sense to me that Johns Hopkins University, one of the premier healing institutions in the entire universe, is in this neighborhood surrounded by extreme poverty. I knew there would never be a way to address that unless there was some kind of coalition or collaborative effort that had built some collective power.

ONGOING CHALLENGES FOR
WOMEN AND LOCAL FAITH COMMUNITIES

I guess I really do feel strongly that if people are going to identify as people of faith and the idea that we're here to create Beloved Community and God's will be done on earth as it is in heaven, then this is a moral imperative—to act, to act strategically and collectively.

—Susan Leslie

Although community organizing has the capacity to and sometimes does create change in congregations, the vision for such transformation remains an unfulfilled desire for some women in this work. Tamisha Walker is a formerly incarcerated community organizer in California whose participation in a faith community while in prison transformed her life. Out of gratitude to God for that experience, she longs to be a catalyst for greater faithfulness in congregations around the call to do justice.

After her time in prison, Walker was hired to do research among the formerly incarcerated in the Bay Area of California. The sponsoring organization for the research was a PICO (now Faith in Action) federation, CCISCO of San Francisco. Walker tells how she and her team got connected with churches:

Our team didn't want to organize in churches because we all had made it clear that we had experienced so much pain and rejection from the faith community that we didn't want to organize in that space. But CCISCO's director at that time said, "Well let's help people understand that. You don't necessarily have to organize those people, but help them understand." So we began to tell our stories in different congregations. That became really valuable to me. It was so obvious that people did not understand how to interpret the story of someone who had been incarcerated.

I had agreed to be a part of these conversations because I felt that I shouldn't question whether these were God's people. But I did want to know why these people weren't more sensitive and empathetic and caring. So I started going to the churches and having discussions. There's this sense of respectability and this whole judging thing of someone's past. That was very present. It was like, "Oh, you committed a crime? You went to jail? Well, you should have! Now you need to be saved because you're a sinner!" Good thing God had already saved me while I was in jail!

I knew that a lot of it was fear; they were afraid of us. The other thing was shame. I found out a lot of them had family members who were incarcerated and some of them had even been arrested and incarcerated themselves, for things they were ashamed of. It was fear, shame, and judgment preventing these congregations from being fully invested to work on these issues.

I went through this whole back and forth with God, asking, "What am I supposed to be doing with all of this for you, Lord, and for the Body of Christ?" I felt like maybe, through the organizing we do and policy work and infrastructure shifts and reinvestment and narrative change and who we are when we return from prison, we could overcome all of this fear, shame, and judgment that still exists in the church.

I feel in some way responsible for the faith community really getting this piece around their own shame and fear and judgment that prevents them from showing up; not just for people who have been incarcerated, but for the community around their churches and the community within their churches. Because there's a lot of hurt there. But they don't know each other's stories. They've been in the congregation together for a long time, but don't necessarily feel they can confide in each other.

Just for example, the foreclosure crisis was huge for certain PICO congregations in California. You had people from the churches marching in the streets and in front of Wells Fargo. But even that was still comfortable. When you start asking people to take action for "the undeserving," then it's a whole different ballgame. Now you have to challenge the values and the thinking of the church. These are not things that churches are extremely comfortable about getting out there and marching about!

Do we wait on the church to change or do we go straight to the people who are in pain and figure out how to get them to take action, to empower them? Maybe it's not one or the other; I don't know.

I have my own lament about congregational life. Without question, these are times of dramatic statistical decline in worship attendance, with a sharp increase of the religiously unaffiliated in the United States. But most congregations seem determined either to hang on to their self-serving status quo, likely into obscurity, or else to keep trying the next "flavor of the month" in terms of growth programs or maintenance strategies.

Despite the vision and work that organizers and church leaders might generate to use organizing as a catalyst for change inside of congregations, that process can be painfully slow, with scant evidence, at times, that it is actually happening. Leah Wiley is Director for Training and Development for the DART national organizing network. Affiliates in DART challenge their leaders to work toward turning out, to their annual Nehemiah public actions, the equivalent of their average weekly worship attendance. The goal is not only to boost participation in the action, but also to more deeply instill the principles of organizing and the value of its public issues into the life of the congregation. I asked Leah whether this plan was having the desired effect in congregations that are a part of DART affiliates:

> I have to say I don't think so. The other congregational culture—of people being on committees and certain people being in charge of certain aspects, and the priority of coming to church on Sundays and hearing the choir sing and tossing a few bucks in the plate—that's so ingrained! It's true in whatever demographic or denomination.
>
> It's still a goal, though, and clergy who are committed to it see that vision. But it's so hard to break the other prevailing culture in congregations. I have yet to see that culture shifted from the old to the new in any significant way.

I'm not so naïve as to consider community organizing a cure for decline; though in some cases I've seen and heard about how congregations that engage with it do grow or revitalize. I do, however, view organizing as a particularly faithful way of life that brings renewed spiritual meaning to people of faith, and God-blessed, justice-oriented neighborliness to congregations.

Doran Schrantz holds out that same hopefulness when she describes the sort of conversion she experienced when she first came into congregation-based community organizing:

> My first six months I spent time following a senior organizer around, going to a bunch of suburban White churches. And at the time I was feeling like I didn't really like these people. I wondered where all the "good and righteous, justice-seeking people" were!
>
> I had a profound moment, though, after meeting with a woman who seemed old to me, and she wasn't very educated, and the conversation we were having caused me to wonder what I was doing with these people that I was trying to get away from! But I was really agitated by that. I wondered why I was so judgmental.
>
> I realized that these were exactly the people I needed to be organizing and working with! And I felt at peace with that afterwards. It felt like, if I believe

in this thing about democracy, and that faith and that people have this capacity, where else would I go? What else would I do? It didn't make sense to leave.

Mary Lim-Lampe tells about how being a part of a congregation provides her with a strong foundation for the public organizing work she does:

> Moving to California, I'm around more unchurched people than I have been my whole life. You even have to be careful about saying you're a church person, because people will dismiss you for that, as someone who doesn't have a critical thought.
>
> But it has been my faith and my belief in prayer and worship that has given me the armor to deal with this stuff around "resist." It doesn't hurt me as much as I've noticed it hurts other people. I think this study and spiritual practice I've had has helped me feel armed.

Melissa Reed, whose vocation is grounded in the congregation and non-profit community where she is pastor and co-organizer, finds her hope for the church and the world through organizing:

> Organizing opened up my eyes to see things and understand things in ways I never had before, and I could never not know those things again! Alone, though, you can't do anything significant about those things. But the collective gives you the ability, the relationships, the freedom to look at those things and not be in despair, but actually perhaps respond. It's in the experience that we have in community, the liberation in the struggle, where I find hope.
>
> My soul is integrated when I'm organizing with people. The outcomes become less critical, though we need to keep chipping away and trying for change. But I don't think the hope of a vision of something we could accomplish is winning in itself; it's the fact that we have community and authenticity and life. Revelry as resistance is important. This, now, is where my hope comes from.

I'm not giving up on congregations as essential spaces in our communities and culture. I owe too much to my own upbringing in vital congregations, and to those local faith communities I've been a part of in my adult life that foster healthy spirituality with a real connection to the Divine. Besides, practically speaking, congregations are among the few remaining organized social gathering spaces where at least the rhetoric and often the reality of radical inclusion—including the leadership of women—is demonstrated. That is no small thing!

Chapter Three

The Transformation of
National Religious Bodies

Mordecai said to Esther, "If you keep silence at such a time as this, relief
and deliverance will rise from another quarter. . . . But perhaps you have
come to royal dignity for just such a time as this." Esther replied, "I will go
to the king, though it is against the law; and if I perish, I perish." (Esther
4:14, 16b)

QUEEN ESTHER: DELIVERER OF HER PEOPLE,
PRESERVER OF A POWERFUL FAITH TRADITION

The book of Esther is in the Hebrew Scriptures (the Christian Old Testament).
The story takes place at a time in history when the people of Israel are living in
exile in Persia. The book is named for the story's protagonist, a young Jewish
woman whose older cousin and legal guardian Mordecai strategizes to get the
King of Persia to select Esther as his next queen. This happens after the king
has dismissed the reigning queen because of her disobedience to one of his
commands.

Shortly after Esther is selected as queen, her cousin Mordecai angers the
king's top advisor Haman by refusing to bow down to him when he passes by, as
the king has commanded all his subjects to do. Haman learns that Mordecai's re-
fusal is based on his identity as a Jew. So, rather than punish Mordecai alone for
his disobedience, Haman plots to have all the Jews living in Persia destroyed.
Unaware that Queen Esther is herself a Jew, Haman convinces the King, also
unaware of her religious identity, to issue a decree calling for the annihilation
of the entire Jewish people on a certain day in the near future.

Once the decree is issued, and as panic begins to spread among the Jews,
Mordecai sends word to his cousin Esther to appeal to the king on her people's
behalf. At first Esther declines Mordecai's request, citing a law forbidding
anyone to enter the king's chambers without being summoned, on threat of

death. But Mordecai argues that Esther will eventually be killed anyway, if the decree to destroy all the Jews is carried out. His final appeal to her is this: "Who knows? Perhaps you have come to royal dignity for just such a time as this." So, Esther relents and vows to approach the king, though it is against the law, saying, "If I perish, I perish."

After observing a three-day fast, and, through Mordecai, asking the same of the Jews throughout the land, Esther dresses in her royal robes and cautiously enters the king's throne room. Upon seeing her, we read that, "she won his favor and he held out to her the golden scepter that was in his hand," indicating that she is welcome to come forward. Then the king asks her what it is that she needs from him, promising to give her whatever she asks.

After a series of what seem like stalling tactics on Esther's part, a few days later she reveals to the King the plot that Haman has concocted to have Esther's entire race eradicated, of course also revealing her own religious identity. Angry that he has been fooled into signing such a decree, the King condemns Haman to death, installs Esther's cousin Mordecai as Haman's successor in the role of high counsel, and writes a new decree allowing the Jews to defend themselves from the death squads that already have been deployed throughout the kingdom.

Because of Esther's courage and advocacy, Haman's plot to annihilate the Jewish people is thwarted. However, as the Jews seek to defend themselves according to the king's new decree, they kill tens of thousands of Persians who had sought to carry out Haman's initial order.

TRANSFORMING RELIGIOUS TRADITIONS

The story told in the book of Esther is an example of how women throughout history have been agents of transformation within the context of their broader religious traditions. According to this story, had it not been for Esther and the organizing she and Mordecai did, the entire Jewish population living in Persia would have been destroyed. Esther's advocacy led to the saving of her people and her religious tradition, which is celebrated on an enduring holiday, Purim, a favorite of Jewish people to this day.

On a more somber note, religious scholars also recognize the threatened destruction of the Jewish population in Persia at the time of this telling as one of many occasions throughout history when Jews have been subjected to racial hatred and the threat of genocide. Esther prevented such an outcome, securing the survival of her people and their religious heritage. Still, the killing of so many Persians in order to stop the genocide of the Jews is another tragic subtext of this story.

Using the principles of community organizing, women continue to participate in the transformation of their broader religious traditions in the current era. Certain national faith bodies—sometimes referred to as denominations—

have undergone significant transformation because of the incorporation of community organizing principles, utilized particularly by women. This chapter points to how this has occurred in three denominations. But I begin by highlighting the strategies of an organization that has brought various faith traditions together around a common commitment to community organizing.

The Interfaith Organizing Initiative (IOI)

> To be in a multi-racial, multi-faith setting like that, where people are very strategic and really faith-rooted in their approach to justice, meant that I gained so much sophistication and understanding and it enabled me to be more influential at the level I was at. Just being with those kinds of people, strategizing together as to how we can really scale up this whole field, working on messaging together, that sort of thing. Just to have other people like you who were direct peers in the same positions, to compare notes and support each other. It was IOI that got me to see myself as someone who could be part of moving a whole denomination. I wouldn't have thought of myself that way before.
>
> —Susan Leslie

During my tenure as Director for Congregation-based Organizing for the Evangelical Lutheran Church in America (ELCA), I have participated in a national organization comprised of executive-level elected leaders, along with national staff members who hold positions similar to mine in their own faith bodies. This is the Interfaith Organizing Initiative (IOI). At the time I was most active, ten faith bodies participated, seven of which were Christian, two that were Jewish movements, and the Unitarian Universalist Association. Members also included organizing practitioners from congregations representing their various faith traditions, funders interested in supporting faith-based organizing, high-level representatives from the national organizing networks, and faculty from a few theological seminaries.

Founded in 2003 by Rev. Mark Hanson, then Presiding Bishop of the ELCA, and Dr. William Shaw, then President of the National Baptist Convention, USA, the IOI was established to advance two main goals: (1) deepen our institutional and congregational capacities to be more powerfully engaged in public life for the sake of justice; and (2) develop processes and strategies for building power necessary to win policy changes that expand justice at the national level.

Faith Bodies Get S-T-R-A-T-E-G-I-C

While I was serving on the coordinating committee and then as chair of the IOI, my interfaith counterparts and I established what we called our

S-T-R-A-T-E-G-I-C approach to achieving the organization's goals, especially regarding capacity-building. Each letter of the acronym represents a
key concept. We determined that, by working to strengthen each of these
concepts, our faith bodies, their congregations, and their members would
be more effective agents of divine justice in society.

The "S-T" in strategic stands for *S*upport from the *T*op. My denomination's
Presiding Bishop and the President from the National Baptist Convention
already had demonstrated their support for organizing by establishing the IOI
and engaging with various organizing networks. Prior to this move, in 2001,
then Presiding Bishop of the ELCA Rev. H. George Anderson had authorized
the establishment of a national Director for Congregation-based Organizing
to work out of its Church in Society division. That first Director was my
predecessor, Rev. Terry Boggs. Only two other national faith bodies, the
Union for Reform Judaism and the Unitarian Universalist Association, had
full-time directors charged with infusing denominational DNA with organizing principles. We in the IOI wanted to maintain and deepen the support of
top officials who were already on board, as well as develop similar support
in the other member denominations.

The "R" in strategic stands for *R*ecognition. The idea here is that it's
important to get the word out among the rank and file of the denomination,
and beyond, about the valuable role faith-based community organizing
plays. So IOI members worked to get articles about organizing written and
printed periodically in our own denominational publications. We called
attention to publicity that appeared in the secular press when our leaders
and congregations were involved in public arena issue work. We urged our
data-collecting branches to keep track of who and how many of our leaders
and congregations were joining organizing efforts, and any statistics they
could gather and share about how that was affecting congregational life and
member participation.

The "A" in strategic stands for the *A*llocation of funds. We in the IOI
understood, from our training and from practical insight, that one of the
components of power and influence is money. Granted, our churches and
denominations never seem to have enough of it; but we were determined that
more of it would be directed toward community organizing efforts than had
traditionally been the case. Our denominations each had played a significant
role in the development of various social services and organizations, including hospitals, schools, and refugee resettlement efforts, along with myriad
food pantries, shelters for the homeless, and some community development
programs. Clear that organizing is a vital but often underused tool in the justice toolbox, we committed ourselves to directing significant denominational
dollars to the field.

The "T" in strategic stands for *T*raining. In full accord with our organizing network partners, we understood the importance of getting more and more leaders in our congregations and institutions trained in the tools and principles of organizing. One of the best ways we knew of doing that was to promote the excellent training programs of all of the organizing networks, providing scholarships when possible to defray the cost for those who needed that type of assistance. Many of us also supplemented network trainings with our own introductory events, or worked with our theological seminaries to expose leaders in formation to the field.

The "E" in strategic stands for (mid-level) *E*xecutives. It's great to have top-of-the-pyramid support for organizing, and equally important that support be fostered among those who serve in mid-level executive positions throughout the organization. That might include regional bishops, district presidents or superintendents, professional staff members who work at those same levels, elected lay leaders on regional councils, and so on. Building relationships with, orienting, and training leaders at those levels helps assure that the principles of organizing get implemented strategically and disseminated out more broadly within the faith body.

The "G" in strategic stands for *G*rounded in the sacred texts and theological foundations of each faith tradition. Often the argument against congregations getting involved in organizing is that it's not the central role of faith communities to be active in the public arena, beyond doing charity. Along this line of thinking, faith communities should focus on their worship life and on the spiritual formation of their members. To counter this tendency, it's imperative to highlight the significant stories and major thematic threads running through our sacred texts and faith traditions that have to do with God's pursuit of justice and the divine call to human agents to join in that pursuit.

The "I" in strategic stands for *I*ssues. The faith bodies involved in the IOI each have histories and the regular practice of developing public statements on various social issues. Most also have advocacy offices active at state and national levels working in support of public policy that reflects the positions of those social statements. The IOI's commitment was to link that advocacy work with the grass-roots mobilization, leadership development, and public action efforts that the various organizing networks were leading, to strengthen the involvement of and the impact made on those most affected by unjust public policy.

The "C" in strategic stands for *C*ollegiality. A key to the effectiveness of community organizing is power in numbers—the power of the collective—which is built in part on the cultivation of peer relationships. The IOI worked toward the development of collegial support systems among clergy, laity, professional staff, and elected denominational leaders. Those systems also contribute to a more broadly shared ownership of the role of organizing in the faith body, as well as a level of accountability that keeps the system active, growing, evolving, and true to its faith foundations and values. So:

S-T   *Support from the Top*
R   *Recognition*
A   *Allocation of funds*
T   *Training*
E   *Executives*
G   *Grounded in sacred texts and theological foundations*
I   *Issues*
C   *Collegiality*

During the time that I was most active in the organization, members of the IOI met at least annually in person, and through conference calls and other virtual meeting approaches several additional times during the year. At each gathering we focused on various aspects of the S-T-R-A-T-E-G-I-C formula, sharing best practices, troubleshooting challenges, conducting workshops, inviting speakers and panels, all in order to make progress in each of our denominations toward those goals.

Several national faith bodies have worked intentionally to incorporate the principles and practices of organizing into their denominational DNA in ways that follow this S-T-R-A-T-E-G-I-C approach. Three of these faith traditions in particular have undergone significant transformation due to the leadership of powerful women.

American Judaism

Forming Congregational Leaders

Jeannie Appleman is a Modern Orthodox Jewish lay woman who has changed how rabbinical students are formed into leaders. In 2006, with a grant from the Nathan Cummings Foundation, Appleman started the Seminary Leadership Program. She had been a community organizer for many years, and then a funder of faith-based community organizing through Jewish Funds for Justice (now Bend the Arc). Through her and her colleague Rabbi Jennie Rosenn's relational connections, Appleman persuaded officials in several rabbinical schools from various Jewish traditions to promote a cross-movement course in the theology, principles, and practices of community organizing. Twelve years into the project, which has expanded beyond seminaries, Appleman reflects:

> We've trained probably 500 rabbis and religious educators, in the seminaries and through our fellowship program and through these other trainings that we do. The thing I really want to get across about the seminary program that is so

different, and why it works, is that it looks at organizing not as a set of skills but a way of operating in the world. So we teach these rabbis to use organizing in the myriad different ways that you can use it inside any context, whether it's a synagogue or a school or a non-profit or as a chaplain. To me that's the difference. It's not just one more social justice program.

A concept that has become most important is the relational aspect. The practice of relationship building is transforming Jewish communities where the rabbis we train are going. Many of our rabbis start their rabbinates with one-to-ones. One of them did 100 in the first 90 days. It completely transformed how he was going to do his work.

The other key concept has been the Iron Rule, "Never do for someone what they can do for themselves." It's having a huge effect on synagogues that have become so fee-for-service oriented. The Iron Rule is radical in that setting. We did a listening campaign in one particular synagogue, where the staff was doing everything. We engaged 150 people in a particular demographic. They cooked up all kinds of things that they wanted to do as a synagogue! Now they are shifting the thinking of some other pockets within the congregation. How a board functions can change; membership committees do one-to-ones instead of surveys. We have to help people see that they needn't look at demographic studies to determine what programing they should provide; they can do that through listening to their own congregants!

Action is the other fundamental. Synagogues become social clubs. If you have relationality without action, it's a social club. If you claim a set of values, which all congregations do, you have to operationalize those values, or you're missing the point. That's the other agitation that we're doing with rabbis. Sometimes they're so deeply engaged in learning and spirituality that they're not even asking the question about justice work. Yet justice is one of the tenets of their mission statement! So the agitation is, "How is this synagogue showing up in the world?" The Torah is not just this document and this spiritual practice. If the Torah isn't walking you to the public square, outside the four walls of your synagogue, then something important is missing.

Through Appleman's efforts, American Judaism has fully embraced the second "T" in the S-T-R-A-T-E-G-I-C formula, by bringing community organizing training into the center of its clergy and lay leadership development processes. This of course has required a significant financial investment on the part of the denomination and its partner institutions, satisfying the A-for-Allocation-of-funds part of the formula. And her efforts have required leaders in formation to dig deeply into their theological *G*rounding, by incorporating into their trainings careful scriptural and traditional exploration of the centrality of justice and action in Judaism.

Rallying Jews Statewide

Stephanie Kolin, a self-described product of the system that Jeannie Appleman established, is a rabbi in the Reform tradition. Kolin spent several years between congregational rabbinates as the co-director of Just Congregations, the community organizing strategy of the Reform Movement. As part of that work, she co-founded and directed Reform California, the first-ever campaign of California Reform congregations to act together on issues of common concern. It was in some ways an experiment, but on a large, state-wide scale, to show just how influential this particular movement in Judaism could be in the world when we work in partnership across lines of difference. Here's Kolin's account of that effort:

What became really clear to me was that the rabbis, the cantors, the lay leaders, they wanted more power than they had being one congregation alone. They wanted to have a greater impact, be more effective, all of it. And they kept getting stymied by state problems because they had no statewide power. So we started to dream together. We have a hundred congregations in California! We started meeting with our colleagues starting in L.A. We started asking why people cared about justice. We started doing text study together and dreaming this thing into existence.

In the meantime, I'm meeting with some people up north, because this isn't supposed to be L.A. alone. So I'm talking to some rabbis up there and we decide we are going to ask their colleagues whether something like this might matter to them. They talked to something like 500 colleagues and the question they asked them was, "What is the California that you dream of, and what is your lived experience that has gotten you to that dream?" They went and talked to all these colleagues and started to hear everything that you could imagine: education, immigration, health care, transportation, everything.

So this team decided it was time to call the question. A dozen from the L.A. team flew up to Burlingame and met with a bunch of their colleagues for a full day, and we got an expert who could tell us about politics in California. We had some funders in the room because we knew this was going to take money.

We had a full day together, talking about why we do this work, what it means to do it together vs. feeling alone and isolated from each other. We talked about the issues that matter to us. We did this teaching about the political landscape. I did a training about what it means to work in coalition with others. We did a brief training on research meetings because that was what was going to happen next.

When the time came, one of the leaders from L.A. called the question: "Should we do this?" We went around the room and it was unanimous! Let's do this, join together, build a statewide organization of Reform Jews. One rabbi testified that she had felt very alone up until this moment, taking risks on justice issues. "But to know that this room of people, that my colleagues are going to have my back? I've never felt like that before. We should do this!" It was really exciting.

That day people signed up in pairs to do research meetings. We did 30 meetings. Before each meeting I would get on the phone with the leaders and put together an agenda. They'd go off and have the meeting, then come back and share what they learned. I was at some of the meetings, but not most. The research meetings were with experts in the field, legislators, coalition leaders, and academics. (We wanted to understand the wonky-ness behind some of the issues we were researching.)

It came down to about five possible campaigns. We had a regional gathering in Palm Springs. They got 100 people into the room, their colleagues. They suggested that we call ourselves Reform California. They presented the five campaign proposals to test them out. We recorded what they cared about, their stories. Ultimately the first campaign decided on was to be on immigration.

We had found that there was a potentially winnable campaign around the TRUST Act, which someone already had on the legislative agenda. There was a federal law on the books that said that if you were arrested, your fingerprints were taken and sent to the FBI, who would then send them to ICE [Immigration and Customs Enforcement.] If you looked suspicious, ICE would fax the jail and ask that the person be held until they could come and get them and start deportation. The TRUST Act would mean that, when that fax came in, the people running the jail would say "No." Once you did your time or paid your fine, you were released. You weren't there waiting for ICE to come.

This practice, of being under threat of ICE custody, had kept all kinds of people, victims of crimes, victims of domestic abuse, witnesses to crimes, from coming forward. We got into this campaign and threw in everything we had, working with the TRUST Act Coalition. We were working with the Asian Law Caucus, the National Day Laborers Organizing Network, and PICO California, the top leaders of the coalition. They were amazing and they were so eager to draw us in. Ultimately, we brought sixty people to Sacramento to lobby. Great stories came out of that. When Jews show up to lobby, the immediate assumption is that we're there to talk about Israel. And here we were, talking about immigration!

The TRUST Act passed the legislature eventually. It had been vetoed by the governor three times previously, though. And we had every reason to believe that he would veto it again. It was on his desk when the High Holy Days rolled around.

We decided to enact a strategy of asking our rabbis to preach about this on Rosh Hashanah and to ask their congregants to break the switchboard at the governor's office. In one congregation, one congregant who had a particular relationship with the governor heard about this and was appalled that this anti-immigrant legislation was happening in his state. He got us a meeting with the governor, and he got on that call with the rabbi and they had basically seven minutes with him.

That, plus the 1,000 phone calls we put in, plus all the work we had done, plus, especially, the three years of the interfaith coalition's work before us, plus the Latino community showing up for so many years and sitting on the floor of the Governor's office until this was done—on October 5, 2013, we won. And I just started weeping.

The efforts that Kolin spearheaded among Reform Jews in California relates to the S-T-R-A-T-E-G-I-C formula in a couple ways. Perhaps most obvious is that the coalition they formed went right from organizing as Reform California to picking an *I*ssue and joining a coalition on an issue campaign to pass a statewide bill. But what also comes through in Kolin's narrative is that the leaders involved experienced a significant level of *C*ollegiality in the process. Rabbis from around the state of California were building relationships with each other, joining together in acts of justice, and feeling supported in the work they felt called by God to do.

The Evangelical Lutheran Church in America (ELCA)

Running an Action on One's Own Denomination

The IOI's main intent was to bring the tools and principles of organizing more fully into congregational life for the purpose of getting more congregations and leaders involved in the work of justice in the public arena. But these same tools and principles can change the nature of a national faith body internally, when its own journey toward being a just institution is hanging in the balance. What follows is a case where the "I" in S-T-R-A-T-E-G-I-C came sharply into focus as an internal issue campaign within a national faith body. Other aspects of the formula are also evident in the narrative.

In August of 2009, the Evangelical Lutheran Church in America (ELCA) changed its policy of prohibiting "sexually active" gays and lesbians from serving as pastors. Emily Eastwood was a pivotal leader in bringing about this change, serving as the Director for the Reconciling in Christ (RIC) program of Lutherans Concerned, the central organization leading in this effort. It took many years of work and numerous failed attempts before the new policy was adopted by the ELCA's governing assembly of voting members. Eastwood credits her training in organizing, in part, for the eventual success of this years-long campaign.

As RIC Director, I went around the country—34 synods the first year, eighteen more than once. That first year we were "identifying and developing" around a strategic plan that would move more congregations forward to becoming publicly welcoming [of gays and lesbians]. I would go to Lutherans Concerned chapters or congregations that had invited me. I would give a presentation on the RIC process and then would look for people to rally around our shared self-interest. The second year was focused on "training for action." The trainings were in three parts, the first being faith-based community organizing. I wanted to organize a core team in every synod in the ELCA to work on RIC. The final step was to "evaluate and re-vision."

Besides following our vision, there were some catalyzing moments for the movement. 2007 was the year of the Bradley Schmeling trial. The jury or discipline committee overseeing the process said that the current policy [of excluding sexually active gays from ordained ministry] was wrong! But he could still be removed from the clergy roster pending the results of the 2007 vote at the Assembly [about gay pastors.] That same year, inspired by the Schmeling case, we had clergy coming out of the closet in a press-embargoed event, coming out all together at the national Churchwide Assembly, 82 of them.

When the policy didn't change in 2007, we had back-up resolutions. One was to give bishops permission to not discipline "out" pastors, and that resolution passed. But Bradley's bishop chose to discipline anyway, even though he had discretion not to. He decided to press charges. We knew then that this was it. Because Bradley was "Rosa Parks" for our movement. He was pristine, he had been out, he had been honest, he was beloved by his congregation, which was ready to go to the mat for him. He was well-known across the movement, a fabulous preacher, a winning, genuine personality. He didn't want to be the poster boy for policy change. He just wanted to be out and open about his relationship with another ELCA pastor.

I did a lot of relationship building in those years with people in positions of power in the ELCA. I found out a lot about people, informing my work, giving me insight into these people that I wouldn't otherwise have. We continued our trainings. We began meeting with leaders working on the ELCA's developing study and eventual social statement on sexuality. We had people building relationships with those folks. We also went to Conference of Bishops' meetings to build relationships, meet between their sessions and over lunch, that sort of thing. We got really smart. We had professional parliamentarians on our legislative team. We trained voting members to do memorials at synod assemblies, passing them over the objection of memorial committees, even.

We needed the social statement on sexuality that would be voted on at the 2009 Assembly to have certain parameters, and also the continuing resolutions that followed. We had done trainings of voting members, we ran a press strategy, we knew what we were doing. We had professionals on our staff around media issues.

We had developed a devotional booklet that was beautifully done; not confrontational, but relational, where our members would go and sit down with people and have conversations. It was based in one-to-one visits and storytelling. We'd get people to relate from below the neck, asking people about their favorite Bible passages, sharing our own. We had a whole voting member training session on using scripture—passages of their own choice—to demonstrate that we are lovers of scripture, contrary to our opponents' rhetoric.

In the end, the social statement, which required a two-thirds majority, passed with one extra vote. And the continuing resolutions, which essentially changed policy regarding the ordination of gays and lesbians, also passed.

With this 2009 policy change, the ELCA became one of a growing body of religious denominations that allow for and celebrate the ordination of LGBT clergy. In 2013 the ELCA's Southwest California Synod elected the denomination's first openly gay, partnered bishop. At the time of this writing, the first openly transgender ELCA pastor has just been ordained. Through the organizing efforts that Emily Eastwood and her colleagues and allies began, more and more congregations are welcoming the gifts of LGBT pastors, and more and more LGBT members are affirmed and supported by clergy who share similar sexual identity journeys.

Changing the Way We Do Church

Community organizing is gaining a greater foothold in the ELCA as more and more of its leaders and congregations understand the merits of utilizing organizing tools and principles. But it's also getting harder for leaders to sustain their congregations, as a myriad of cultural shifts threaten the viability of traditional as well as innovative approaches to doing ministry.

Meghan Sobocienski is a Lutheran Deacon, trained as a community organizer, who served for four years as Coordinator of the ELCA's Organizing for Mission Cohort. As ELCA Director for Organizing, I founded the Cohort in 2010 in order to bring pastors and congregational leaders together who were intentionally employing the tools and principles of community organizing to start new churches or redevelop existing ministries. I recognized that this was cutting-edge church work that was relatively rare in our denomination, and that its practitioners needed support from their peers and the national office in order be effective in their efforts.

The Cohort began with a retreat in the summer of 2010, gathering fifteen leaders representing five Lutheran ministries from various locations around the country. Sobocienski was among them, along with her husband, Pastor John Cummings. Together they were starting a new worshiping community with mostly Latino immigrants in Southwest Detroit. By 2012 the Cohort had grown so that we were hosting twice-annual three-day gatherings and attracting between 30–50 participants, representing up to 20 different ministries.

Because my role as Director for Congregation-based Organizing included many other duties besides coordinating the Cohort, I brought Sobocienski on as its half-time, deployed staff coordinator, with the vision of continuing to grow its membership and activities. I also understood that this was a movement that was attracting young leaders and leaders of color in ways that few of our denomination's efforts were accomplishing. To continue doing so, a leader younger than I, with closer ties to communities of color, was needed to coordinate it.

Sobocienski has since passed the Cohort Co-Coordinator baton on to two young female colleagues, Bianca Vazquez and Kristen Kane, who, in addition to coordinating the Cohort, work part-time out of Luther Place Memorial Church in Washington, D.C., a Cohort member congregation. Here Sobocienski reflects on her time as a member and as Cohort Coordinator in terms of the impact it has had on her and her husband's ministry and on our denomination:

It's always been a super valuable network of people; and they're the only people John and I know of in the church that we can actually draw on about everything from, "How do you do this?" to "Why did this thing happen?" and understanding political and race dynamics and who we are personally. We don't want just sympathizers, but people who will push us to grow.

I remember being so excited about and enjoying the organizing I did with PICO, but I felt like there wasn't a huge integration of faith in that work. It was so linear and I don't experience the Holy Spirit that way! There was often no room for the Holy Spirit. But in the Cohort, it was so Spirit-led and at the same time intentional about building power for the sake of changing institutions and structures and then the world, as a result. It was great to get my brain stretched in those early years of the Cohort.

As far as how the Cohort has been significant for the ELCA, the model of not having the coordinator(s) as full-time staff at the national office, that really matters. Instead, having people on the ground, in congregations part-time and working with the larger institution part-time, is key.

Also, the participatory budgeting process we developed is really important, having members of the Cohort share in it and be transparent, rather than the guardedness of the national office. The way that you, Sue, understood what is centralized and what is de-centralized was significant; what we could do on our own vs. what we needed to funnel through higher institutional channels. You held a lot of inside conversations in order to create little pockets of independence for us. You advocated for dollars centrally but then trusted the grass-roots people with you to determine exactly where that money would be spent. You didn't have to control it, and that was unusual within the denomination.

Then, the gatherings are planned considering the context where we're going to meet; that's where we start. We ask, "What does the context need that we can bring and what does the context bring that we need as ministries?"

The entire ELCA is siloed around race. That serves only a few people who can keep making decisions they've always made. That keeps people pitted against each other and unable to organize. There's no attention being paid to the common dynamics of the various diversities. And that behavior benefits certain populations in power.

It also benefits certain traditionally marginalized groups because some of them can get perks from the organization to keep building their silos. It keeps the whole dysfunctional system alive and well. And it allows White leaders to continue to feel guilty so that we remain immobile so that we don't work for change.

The Cohort tries to embody what the various diversities mixed into the denomination have in common. We try to bring parts of the siloed institution together. In the Cohort we bring a space where people gather from across the various ethnic and cultural silos and strategize about how to create more equity as a church, and power and healing in the world, starting with our neighborhoods of context.

As far as what happened on my watch as Cohort coordinator, that first Chicago meeting after I came on was pivotal. We were starting to bring church theologians into the room around that time to accompany us. And we were seeing more leaders of color and their proven allies joining with us. We also were seeing incredible leadership in certain of those newer leaders. We were open to let their truths be heard, around racial dynamics. We intentionally worked on who to invest in and when. Those were the right people at that time to invest in. Then our decisions started to flow through thinking about each leader and what truth of theirs needed to be shared.

I spent a lot of time on phone one-to-ones with people in the Cohort between meetings. I tried to hold myself to the same accountability I'd learned in PICO, to do ten one-to-ones a week (since I was half-time.) Part of that was just out of a sense of discipline, but it was also about a need to hold the group together. If someone got pissed off, I felt I needed to go after them and find out what was going on.

Part of that was that I felt we weren't always clear about the external vision, so I was trying to keep an evolving structure running. It was always confusing as to whether we were trying to build something inside the institution to change it or building something external to the institution. Those questions became somewhat paralyzing. We tried to do some actions internally—like the new starts metrics work and the access-to-money group. Eventually we settled with being an entity within the ELCA that was modeling what we hoped the ELCA could become, to some degree, rather than a major change mechanism for the whole institution. So then, for me, it became a bit like pastoring a congregation.

The question I still have is about purpose. Why does the Cohort exist? One thing that John and I understand, though, is that the Cohort is the only entity that we feel we can turn to when we're trying to regain a sense of our own ministry's purpose. I have so much self-interest in connecting with people who are doing unique things. I think of them as unicorns and I want to be talking to unicorns.

I need great conversations that reground and re-center me and make me think creatively about my work. How do we find money to do this work? How do we structure ourselves so that we can do what we need to do? How do we grow what we're doing in ways that are meaningful for our participants? Unicorns are the people we can call who will understand us because they're developing non-traditional ministries too. They will call us out, guide us; they're building functional structures and are building equity in the world. They're really hard to find; they're rare, like unicorns.

I think of the Organizing for Mission Cohort as a long-term experiment within the larger denomination. It's an experiment in how to do the work of the church in a non-traditional way, one that puts justice and the life of the community that surrounds the ministry site into center focus. There are other experiments that my and other denominations are conducting to respond to the cultural challenges and pressures on religious institutions. But the Organizing for Mission Cohort is the only one I am aware of that regularly gathers church leaders who are putting the tools and principles of community organizing to intentional use for the sake of leadership development and the doing of justice in those ministries' broader contexts.

The Unitarian Universalist Association (UUA)

Susan Leslie is a Unitarian Universalist lay woman who serves as her denomination's Director for Advocacy and Witness. On the national staff for 25 years, Leslie has orchestrated a significant transformation in the UUA around how congregations understand their role and call in the world. Here she describes the methodical ways that she and others moved their denomination over a period of several years to embrace organizing as a way of doing faithful ministry:

> After 9/11, we had elected our first Black president of the UUA. He established a whole new staff team that I was a part of, called Advocacy and Witness. Before that I had been part of a team called Faith in Action that was very much about doing training in anti-racism and anti-oppression. While that was very good, we felt like it wasn't moving people toward action and being part of dismantling systems of oppression and working for justice. Sure, we had established lots of study groups where people talked and read about White privilege, but we still were not moving out into action.
>
> We'd done a baseline survey of our 1,000 congregations that established that most of them were focused on service and education. But they were not doing a lot around advocacy, organizing, or what we call public witness. So with a new Advocacy and Witness team, the idea was to build on people getting a higher consciousness around oppression and moving into ways to actually dismantle it. One thing that happened at that time was that a Washington advocacy office was added.
>
> Then I asked if I could be someone who would be more of a field organizer, to get our congregations involved in organizing campaigns; because everything isn't D.C.-based advocacy! And even when it is, it's not just about getting an e-mail in your inbox that's going to get people activated. It's by being in relationship with impacted people in your community.
>
> It came to my attention at about that time that roughly 10 percent of our congregations were already participating in faith-based organizing with the various

networks. That gets people's attention when you can say that 10 percent are already involved! This wasn't because of anything we had done at the UUA, though. It was because of good organizing on the part of the networks who were recruiting our congregations on the local level.

What we did then was identify who those folks were. We got some volunteers to work with the networks to get lists of the UUA congregations that were involved. I had a great key volunteer who was willing to work with me who had a strong background in community organizing. He actually hopped in his VW bus and did some site visits around the country where we had congregations that were very involved. And he and I did some phone interviews.

Our next step was to convene a group of leaders, both clergy and lay from those congregations, to meet the day before our annual General Assembly (GA) began. We had some panels and talked about what was working and what was challenging. We had 75 to 100 people and they were so enthusiastic that they said we needed to have some programing at our next General Assembly about this.

About that same time we started doing some sort of public witness at our General Assemblies, like an LGBTQ march or something like that. So these leaders I had convened said we should be the ones to run the public witness event at the next GA, which was to be in Long Beach, California. We had a great PICO affiliate there, and we could see it would make sense for GA attendees to be part of a local action, to see what this looks like. So we managed to set that up.

They were doing an action around affordable housing. In good creative organizing fashion, they were asking for money that was used for the annual Rose Bowl—when homeless people would typically get picked up and kicked off the streets. They wanted that money to go to affordable housing. And then, to make sure there'd be a good tie-in for people from all around the country, somebody from the national Housing and Urban Development office was invited to be there. And we had my boss, our staff Team Director for our Advocacy and Witness office, take a key role.

At that same Long Beach GA in 2004 we had Mary Gonzales from Gamaliel speak in the plenary. She talked about, "If you want to keep doing Mickey Mouse social justice projects in your congregations, I should just leave the podium. But if you want to know how to really make some change that's impactful, you need to check this [organizing] out." I got to introduce her and told about how congregations who were engaged in this model were some of the most vital congregations in our movement.

Our moderator at the time—who is the highest elected official after our president—was a real enthusiast for all of this and was involved in this herself through the Gamaliel network. So that's how we got Mary Gonzales and how I got some funding to bring her in as a speaker. We also had her do a workshop and we had a couple other workshops from congregations involved in the model.

After that, we kept building on it because we kept getting interest. I recruited a congregation-based community organizing clergy group that would be my advisory group, with a clergy member from every one of our districts to serve on this council. I had these 24 clergy leaders who were meeting by phone three times a year and then gathering for an annual meeting. This was 2005–2006. These were energetic people with lots of different ideas about, for example, doing workshops at our UUA clergy chapter meetings on organizing. And they wanted to bring this into the national gathering again. So one year we had Marshal Ganz speak at GA. [Ganz is a Senior Lecturer in Leadership, Organizing, and Civil Society at the Harvard Kennedy School.] And it became clergy to clergy, sharing the model with their colleagues.

I also developed a handbook so that people could know about it. Folks at the UUA Veatch Program—a major foundation—were very excited about the model. The director at the time was Margie Fine who put me in touch with Jews for Justice who had a really good handbook on congregation-based organizing. They were glad to have us take their handbook and re-write it for UUs, adding our own stories from the field. Veatch set up a fund to help congregations pay their first year of affiliate dues and send people to training, because that was somewhat of a barrier to our congregations getting involved.

We developed a whole model for workshops that our leaders could use and adapt for their own contexts at cluster meetings and chapter meetings and statewide meetings. That's also when we began to get involved with the Interfaith Organizing Initiative. We brought our new moderator—Gini Courter—to the IOI gathering in Tennessee. And as a result, she made sure that we got time at the next GA plenary session for a presentation. She invited us to the UUA board meeting to do some educational workshops on what our congregations were doing in this field. And she basically said to the board, "If you don't know about this, you're not going to know about some of the most exciting work that the congregations you represent are doing."

Over time we've absolutely seen an increase in involvement of congregations in this field. When I first started, about 10 percent were involved in organizing. So I started to map where all the network affiliates were located. Then we found all the UUA congregations that were within 25 miles of each of those affiliates. We got a pretty good list of congregations that weren't involved yet who might potentially get involved. We started inviting leaders from those congregations to workshops and clergy did one-to-one calls with those leaders. We identified probably 100 or more congregations that had the potential to relate to an affiliate.

Now, in 2018, we're up to about 200 UUA congregations that are involved in organizing. That's 20 percent, right? It is! One of our pastors, who was from Reno, Nevada, was at one of our workshops at GA. He got so excited about the model that, when he went back to Reno and found out there wasn't an affiliate there, he started researching the different networks. He ended up working with PICO to start a new affiliate! So our folks have also been a part of sponsoring committees in a few places like that; Tulsa as well, for example.

Throughout Leslie's narrative, I notice that she employed all eight of the IOI's S-T-R-A-T-E-G-I-C approaches as she worked to bring organizing into greater prominence in the UUA. She cultivated relationships with and *S*upport from leaders at the *T*op of the church hierarchy. She published a comprehensive handbook that gave *R*ecognition to the organizing model and lifted up the stories of participating UU congregations. She collaborated with Veatch, her denomination's partner foundation, to assure greater *A*llocation of funds for the work. She and her leadership team conducted *T*raining and worked with mid-level *E*xecutives to spread the word about organizing. Although her narrative above doesn't make reference to it, I was aware while a colleague of Leslie's that she and her leaders made frequent reference to the UUA's seven core Principles and six key Sources as they went about their work, thereby *G*rounding all they did in their spiritual tradition. They incorporated *I*ssue campaigns into the ways that they activated leaders and congregations, especially at the annual General Assemblies. And they built systems of *C*ollegiality, starting with the representative advisory board that Leslie put into place early in her strategy.

Leslie's work not only led to the increase in UUA congregations involved in organizing. It also changed how the national office functions and how it relates to its congregations. According to Leslie:

> The denomination itself has shifted in its character to understand itself as an organizing promoter. That's really the hot topic right now, and that's a huge culture shift. We used to have a lot of people saying congregations shouldn't be involved in politics, and confusing politics with partisanship. When I came, a lot of our congregations were doing service projects. And people thought of social justice as the passing of statements at our assemblies, or our officers signing onto letters that other groups invited us to sign. But the consciousness around that has changed. We no longer think of social justice in that way.
>
> The idea is taking hold that, to really live out your faith, you need to be really conscious of whole communities; not just our churches as clubs, but what is the situation and who are the people being oppressed? What's your relation to them and how are you going to build Beloved Community with them? We've been able to make that shift. Before that we were clubs! You could come and have a nice discussion about issues. But action wasn't part of that. The national office has a greater role now in fostering communities of action than ever before.

Despite the important changes that Leslie has fostered in her denomination, she is well aware that major challenges continue, in an era when participation in congregational life is decreasing and cultural threats to traditional UU values are increasing. She continues to work on strategies for meeting these significant challenges:

> Along with our sister organization, the UU Service Committee, we decided we needed to really pull together to take on some of the current anti-nearly-

everything rhetoric. We changed our "Standing on the Side of Love Campaign" to "Side with Love," to satisfy our disabilities community. That's focused on people forty and under, UUs who aren't necessarily congregation-based. There are more and more young adult worship "networks" that worship unconventionally, either in terms of when, where, or how. "Side with Love" is working to create meet-ups, gatherings, containers, for that group of people to stay identified as UUs and be part of movement building. A lot of them are activists around racial or climate justice, etc.

We also came up with our "Love Resists" campaign, which is for our congregations. It's about stopping criminalization of communities that have been targeted by the current administration: Muslims, trans folks, immigrants. Rather than trying to do big and broad, we're really looking at site-specific places where we can protect our communities and be part of helping front-line groups build their base, get involved in electoral strategies, etc. We will do some really deep work around faith values as well.

The Unitarian Universalist Association has one thousand congregations across the country. As Leslie is quick to point out, it's a tiny denomination compared to so many others. But she also pointed out to me that most of the organizing network affiliates across the country now have at least one UU member congregation. And those UU leaders tend to take on prominent roles and responsibilities in their organizations. When I think of the UUA in this context, I'm reminded of a quote from Shakespeare's play *A Midsummer Night's Dream*, regarding the character Hermia: "Though she be but little, she is fierce!"

ONGOING CHALLENGES FOR
WOMEN AND FAITH TRADITIONS

Leaders in national religious bodies all are working hard to meet the challenges of what many call a post-denominational, even a post-religious, era. The stories shared above show how three such bodies are intentionally focused on faith-based community organizing as one kind of remedy for meeting those challenges. As the struggle continues, women involved in organizing have their own ongoing critiques of their various faith traditions.

Mary Gonzales is still an active Catholic church-goer, and laments the falling away from the church of some of her adult children and their children. But she has her own gripes with the church tradition she has been a part of all her life, choosing to define her faith on her own terms:

I have an adult relationship with God now. It's no longer that I have to do these 32 things per week to feed this god that had to be fed all day long with these activities: do this, do that, genuflect, this is how you make the sign of the cross, these are the 42 prayers you have to memorize, these are the 42 steps. I've been way beyond that for many years.

I have decided that no matter what happens in the church by humans, they're not going to jolt my faith. I've decided I'm going to ignore all the stupid things. I'm going to define my relationship with God, how I live, how I pray, how I interact, how I do my organizing work, mentoring others. God's not going to punish me for this!

I feel more in control of my own sense of faith and church. It's really a matter of stepping out of that Roman Catholicism I knew all my life and the 9500 things I needed to do to be saved.

Mary Gruber is also a lifelong Catholic. But she has stopped attending services in the last few years, disillusioned by the messages and by the behavior of too many in the church hierarchy:

During this whole time, with all of the turmoil within the Catholic Church and my own struggle with the disgust of it all—to even go to mass and have to listen to a sermon that is either shaming or else just not in touch with the values that I hold—more and more I've been identifying a difference in values from the pulpit than I hold for myself to be true. I miss going to mass, but I can't even bring myself to go because I'm so disgusted with the messaging that comes across now. I grieve a lack of that community. But I can't continue to church shop anymore. My own kids got disgusted long before I did. So I miss seeing my grandchildren baptized, that sort of thing. But I don't blame them.

Melissa Reed is a Lutheran pastor who continues to identify deeply with much of the Lutheran theology that she grew up with and studied in seminary. But her exposure to organizing has led her to expand her theological understandings beyond those of her own tradition. She also brings some criticism as to how even the best of Lutheran doctrine sometimes gets misrepresented:

As Lutherans, in our theology, it's been distilled to be pretty individualistic in practice. Even in our liturgy, though we confess corporately, it's really about our own sins, individually. Even though our baptismal and Eucharistic theology would say that's not the whole story, but still, that's how it gets interpreted. What are people really hearing and experiencing? Then we combine it with American capitalistic individualism. I went to seminary because I had a lens of collectivity, but I got confronted by how broken and disconnected and siloed people are. And how pressured their lives are by systems that don't actually work for them.

Theologically, I've become a liberation theologian. This work takes you out into the world and into relationship with what the world would call poverty, whether that be economic or the poor places of our lives, the wounds and margins of our own lives and communities. Out of relationship there, scripture, theology, start becoming very active.

Resurrection isn't an idea I have about some day. I get to see and participate in it daily. All those words like healing and reconciliation and liberation are actual experiences that, as a good Lutheran, I believe are activated by the Holy Spirit, who is actually working through collective bodies of people; not just individually through my own little heart, but through the collective body, the Body of Christ.

And the Body of Christ is much bigger to me than the church. The Body of Creation; very earthy and incarnational. When I'm with my community, that's an embodiment of Christ, of God, of Wisdom, but it's not the whole. It's the now and the not yet. There's always tension and paradox that stops me from taking myself too seriously, from playing God.

Reed recently has been contemplating what role she might play in the ongoing development of leaders to serve the church that is called into a rapidly changing reality:

Because of my own experience of coming into an organizing congregation for internship and then getting to come back here to serve a call, and being mentored so expertly that whole time, I have agitation in me to try and create those kinds of opportunities for more students. To develop leaders and contribute to pastoral development, integrated and not separate from the development of communities and organizing.

There are young people interested in theological education and mentoring, but they may or may not be called to be pastors or rostered leaders. They certainly aren't called to go into traditional Lutheran bubbles and become good pastors and organizers there. They're already doing ministry on the ground, so why wouldn't you invest in them in their current contexts?

For me, organizing practices need to be integrated into one's leadership. I can't look at ministry without looking through an organizing lens. How I approach everything has that lens to it.

Onleilove Alston did not grow up in a religious home. But an avid reader from an early age, she got it in her head that she wanted to read the Bible when she was about ten years old. When she took up praying and reading the Psalms three times a day, an observant aunt suggested that she go to the Missionary Baptist church near her home. Alston went, by herself, and went up for their altar call. She was baptized the following week and took her first communion shortly thereafter. She describes it as a powerful conversion experience. These days, Alston has some strong words for the Church when it comes to the treatment of women:

The thing is, people complain about the church. If you want the Church to change, go talk to Black women. We're the majority of the Church. If we all just sat down and didn't go, churches would collapse. Across religions, Black

women are the most spiritually active. If you're going to be a faith-based organizer in this day and age, you're going to have to deal with gender. And you're
going to have to deal with Black women in particular.

So part of my work has been trying to bridge the gap. If we're working with
certain denominations that aren't paying their women clergy equitably, or are
not giving them the senior positions that the men get, how can we let that stand?
If we're working with these groups at a national level, do we do an action on
them around these matters?

Alston has made a major shift in her own spiritual journey, in part to get beyond some of the concerns she has with mainstream Christianity:

I've joined the Hebrew Pentecostal Tradition, which is an historic Black church
where you do believe in Jesus, but you also keep the Sabbath. There's some
overlap with my spiritual journey and my organizing journey. When you start
coming to terms with your own power, you start to live more authentically in
other areas. I had wanted to keep Sabbath from when I was a child. It's in the
Bible! There were certain things I wanted to do that didn't align with typical
Christian ways.

One part of stepping into my power is about going to a faith community that
serves me. My church was started by a Black woman 65 years ago. She started
it in her home; now her grandson leads it. They have a justice team. When they
found out what I did, they were excited and joined the work our organization
is doing.

My own frustration with national religious bodies, including my denomination, is that not enough of them prioritize community organizing as a key
approach to doing effective public ministry. In spite of the IOI's work before
and during my tenure as the ELCA's organizing director, faith bodies still
put much higher priority on acts of charity and political advocacy. Regarding
community development, there is a fair bit of attention paid to it in overseas
mission work, but not as much on the domestic scene. Denominations generally assign more staff people to attend to the realms of charity, advocacy,
and development, and direct more denominational and appeal funds in those
directions, than toward organizing. I don't deny that each of these forms of
public engagement help people of faith and religious institutions live out their
call to faithfulness in the world; and that each, to varying degrees, can make
a difference in the lives of neighbors near and far. But the vision that my IOI
colleagues and I had, that our denominations' DNA would be infused with
organizing principles and practices, has not been fully realized, despite the
efforts and gains of powerful women in leadership.

Chapter Four

The Transformation of Community Organizations

When Abigail saw David, she fell at his feet and said, "My lord, do not take seriously this ill-natured fellow, Nabal." (1 Samuel 25:25a)

ABIGAIL: CLEVER AND RESOURCEFUL AMIDST HOT-HEADED MEN

In the twenty-fifth chapter of First Samuel in the Hebrew scriptures is a story that takes place while Saul is the king of Israel. At this time David, who will eventually succeed Saul as king, is serving as a successful military leader in Saul's army. While patrolling with his troops in a region called Carmel, David and his men encounter shepherds tending the flocks of a rich man named Nabal. While spending several days in Nabal's territory, David and his men provide assistance to the shepherds and extra protection for their flocks. Therefore, when a feast day occurs, David considers it appropriate to send a messenger to Nabal asking him to provide them with whatever he may have at hand so that they might celebrate. The messenger goes to Nabal, who is currently in a different part of his territory working among his sheep shearers.

Now Nabal is described by one of his own men as "so ill-natured that no one can speak to him." So instead of granting the request that the messenger conveys, Nabal refuses on the grounds that David and his men could, for all Nabal knows, be runaway slaves. David is so angry when the messenger returns with Nabal's insulting response that he orders four hundred of his men to strap on their swords and go with him after Nabal to kill him and anyone who might be with him.

One of the shepherds who witnesses all of this vitriol runs to Nabal's home and tells his wife Abigail all that has taken place. He testifies to the fine treatment David and his men showed to the shepherds and warns her that David is

79

determined to kill Nabal. Abigail hurriedly gathers a large load of food and wine and leads a delegation out to meet David before he can reach Nabal. Falling at his feet, she pleads for mercy, apologizes for the foolish behavior of her husband, and makes an eloquent argument for why David ought not take revenge on Nabal. She offers all that she has brought with her as a sign of good will.

David praises Abigail for her good sense in intercepting him and thanks her for deterring him from killing Nabal and anyone else who he might have found with him. He receives the gifts she has provided and assures her that he will refrain from the revenge he had planned against Nabal. When Abigail returns home, she tells Nabal, who has also returned, all that has happened regarding David. Her account makes Nabal literally heartsick, and ten days later he dies. The news of Nabal's death finds its way to David, who rejoices that "the LORD has returned the evildoing of Nabal upon his own heart" (25:39b). David sends messengers to Abigail asking her to become his wife. She accepts immediately, leaving the home she shared with Nabal to join David's household.

THE TRANSFORMATION OF COMMUNITY ORGANIZATIONS

Abigail and Nabal participated not only in a marriage, but in the running of a significant organization in their community, one that employed numerous workers and provided needed resources for its neighbors. When their organization came under threat, due to the ill-natured behavior of its chief executive officer Nabal, Abigail acted quickly and decisively to shift the dangerous dynamics and secure her own and their organization's safety from destruction. Abigail exemplified the role that women often play in how organizations function and what is required to sustain them for the long haul.

There are four major national faith-based community organizing networks in the United States, each with numerous local affiliate organizations. DART, Faith in Action (formerly PICO), Gamaliel, and the Industrial Areas Foundation (IAF) all were founded, and directed for most of their histories, by White men. Female directors of local affiliate organizations have been on the rise for several years; but only recently has the first woman and first person of color taken on the role of executive director of one of the national networks, Gamaliel. Despite not occupying the top-level positions, women have always played key roles in the development, growth, and ongoing transformation of the networks and affiliates.

Gender Equity Inside the Organization

I was at MORE[2] for five years. One thing I worked on was the whole "how to treat a woman" thing in a role like this. There were all these men on the board who asked inappropriate things of me regarding health coverage and other negotiations. I feel like I was part of changing the culture of the way that they treated women, and women of color, in the organization. It was so male dominated for so long.

—Mary Lim-Lampe

The early work that persistent women had to address, which is ongoing, was to level various playing fields so that they would be taken seriously—by the men who founded and were hired by their organizations, and by the faith leaders, many of them male clergy, who were leaders in their organizations. Mary Gruber was part of a Gamaliel affiliate first in St. Paul Minnesota and then when they merged with their Minneapolis and St. Cloud counterpart affiliates to form ISAIAH. She reflects on those years when she was an active leader:

It's exhausting to think back on all the fights I fought internally, within the organization. The nature of those fights was about being a White lay woman leader within any of our organizations. It started with our St. Paul affiliate. We went after our organizer insisting that we women were doing all the work, but men were getting all the titled positions and speaking roles and staff was doing all the planning and designing. I felt that I couldn't just continue going along with whatever they were saying, or let someone with a collar on the stage if I did all the work leading up to it.

The other thing that I did was, after going to Advanced Leader Training, I wanted to be part of ISAIAH's clergy agitation table. I had a proposition all lined up and figured out. But I was told no, because I wasn't clergy. So I started my own table. I went to Pamela and asked her to staff it. I wanted a strong leader table, those who were chairing committees, heading core teams, doing the work. And a lot of us were women. We started our own accountability table. There was a ton of learning that happened for all of us. That's what I wanted. I just didn't want to be a pawn or a figurehead. That was a lot of work, but it was very freeing, that I could make this happen.

Tamisha Walker, a formerly incarcerated organizer in Richmond, California, describes what it's been like to relate to leaders, men and women, who seem to see her as somehow less than adequate in the role because of her gender:

I've challenged male clergy on this: sometimes they want to see "the male organizer," after I've met with them. You talk about moving some work forward and then at the end they ask for So-and-So (a man) to give them a call. I have experienced that!

I've learned to build real relationships with the clergy who will actually see me. The clergy who don't have that attitude, my relationship with them is solely transactional.

I also wonder when the conversation is going to start about how women sometimes treat other women that way, not hearing you because it's coming from a woman and not a man.

As she was developing in her leadership capacities as an organizer, and acquiring a vision and appetite for a more central role, Doran Schrantz proposed to the director of her organization that an associate director position be created. He agreed, and Schrantz stepped into that role. Three years later she became one of ISAIAH's three co-directors. She reflects on the dynamics of serving in that situation, and confesses to some of her own collusion in that reality:

Male leadership was privileged, for sure. Some of that is true in society or reflective of it. That manifests in what gets lifted up and valued, what kind of leadership, how people informally relate. You're just never going to be one of the brothers!

The whole time I was one of the co-directors, all the credit was always conferred to the two male co-directors. The assumption was always that they were the brilliant masterminds. It was infuriating, but it was also safe. The buck stopped there.

I had to learn that, to become a real player in the field, I'd have to acknowledge that people were going to get mad and there was going to be conflict.

Onleilove Alston, who worked for PICO (now Faith in Action), made it part of her mission while with the organization to bring some of these dynamics into open conversation among her peers. She believes that these gender-biased attitudes and behaviors inside of organizations, and among their member congregations, reflect a hypocrisy that undermines the public arena work that these organizations champion:

I started to notice, even in the mass incarceration efforts, that we were talking about it as if it was only Black men. But the rates of who is entering prison for the first time, the highest rate is Black women of child-bearing age. So I have brought a gender lens to the Live Free campaign, both here and nationally.

I also started for PICO the Women's Theology of Liberation program to train women clergy and lay leaders and staff in how to come to all the issues we organize around and bring a gender lens to it. And then how, rooted in our various faith traditions, women can grow in leadership. We have congregations that will join a faith-based organization, but don't believe that a woman should stand in a pulpit or even say something at a forum! Too often well-known women in the faith world have to sit aside at events and just the men get to speak. And too often we have women working as organizers, but they're not being paid a living wage! I'm literally seeing female organizers and clergy marching for Fight for Fifteen for fast food workers, and they themselves might not even be making $15 an hour!

I'm just trying to bring a gender lens and make sure we're not ignoring the gender issues of our leaders. A lot of my work with PICO has been helping the organization look at itself and the missed opportunities in any affiliate, where it will be the majority of women in the action.

Mary Gonzales was the only woman on staff when Gamaliel launched in the late 1980s. The organization started out primarily as a training institute, while its founders also went around the country consulting with groups that were interested in starting local affiliates. Getting people to a week of leadership training was a key strategy for building the capacity of local leaders to get an affiliate up and running. Gonzales describes what it was like for her in those early years:

I was at a table with all White men, and I was the only woman and person of color. In 1987 we started weeklong training. I remember the first seven or eight years and the difficulty we had in trying to get other women organizers to do training. Greg wanted to be sure we had a female and a person of color training in every room. I had to learn to do every single session! I ran from room to room. And sometimes we had four rooms. It was insane!

Developing Effective Trainings and Trainers

Being subjected to that kind of pressure may have seemed insane for Gonzales. But it was also likely part of what shaped her into who many consider the most gifted trainer in the field. She set an example for others to sharpen their own training abilities, so that Gamaliel's training program is one of its strongest assets. I asked Gonzales how she developed her uncanny ability in a training setting to so accurately read people and then bring that personal truth into the room without it being humiliating for them:

I had to work on that. It didn't come naturally. A lot had to do with reflecting on my own life and on how incredibly beautiful the organizers who worked with me were. Some of them really kicked my ass, but that's not all they did. They were supportive, they told me what I was good at, they assured me that I would overcome my fears and doubts. They did a lot of things for me.

So I thought about how to do that in a training session, especially if I'm only going to see this person for one day or one week. How do I inspire them and agitate them and hold them up and hold a mirror up to them and make sure that they don't only see ugliness? That they see opportunity and possibilities and not just failure.

I began to figure out that it was working for me! Other organizers were just as tough on people as I was, but then people hated them. People didn't love me, but they wanted me back. They were enjoying this agitation, this push. And I thought, well, that's the magic!

I've trained other organizers to do three things: walk into the room committed that you're going to engage with every single person. Then, you have to agitate people. But remember that agitation is about pushing them around what's good about them. You have to agitate them to behave the way that God intends them to be and not the way society expects them to be. And third, you have to commit to having a really good time with them. You have to have fun with them. It doesn't mean you're telling jokes; it means they have to smell that you are enjoying your interaction with them.

In chapter 1 I described the impact the Gamaliel organization's Ntosake training program for women had on my own development and that of many others. The establishment of this unique training experience is one of the ways that female leaders have transformed the character of this national network. Now into its third decade, Ntosake plays an integral part in Gamaliel's national training programs. It was the Ntosake project that finally galvanized and united female organizers in the network to develop their training capacity. This led to the diversifying of the national training faculty and provided new and powerful female role models for women and men alike who participate in any of Gamaliel's training offerings.

Pamela Twiss, organizing in a Gamaliel affiliate in St. Paul Minnesota at that time, tells about what motivated her, along with several other women, to contribute to the development of Ntosake on the national level:

The only way I could be a trainer was to develop my own training sessions and practice them on a local level. I needed a safe place to practice my training. At the same time, there was a group of active women leaders, along with me, who realized how hard it was for women to identify their self-interest when they'd go to weeklong training. We were sending them and they'd come back and not be able to name their self-interest. We wondered what that was all about.

We decided to start this women's leadership training. We had twenty women who joined this collective for six months. We had goals and monthly day-long trainings and mentoring sessions. We invited in trainers from the national realm. I would do a session sometime during the day, too, and the guest trainer would evaluate me. I just wanted to learn to train. That was my motivation. I also wanted to help these women leaders get clear on self-interest.

This women's leadership effort we were doing in St. Paul had an impact on the development of Ntosake at the national level. We were among those that Mary Gonzales was working with to create that national version.

Mary Gruber was one of the twenty women who partnered with Twiss in the St. Paul effort around women's leadership. Through those local efforts, she became involved in the national push to create Ntosake:

My first Gamaliel weeklong training was one of the worst experiences I'd ever had! I thought the trainers were so disrespectful. And so dismissive. I felt like they pitted all of us against each other. As a White woman, I was a minority in the group. As a lay person I was a minority, etc. We were often pitted one against the other. And I was always passed over by some of the trainers for a clergy person, especially if they were male. I was just pissed off all the time. How is this supposed to be helping me? It was just making me angry. I was just there, and dismissed. I could learn a process and the steps to follow, the techniques. But the gut part was not effective.

That really fueled my passion to be one of the women to start Ntosake. I was in on that with Pamela locally and Mary on the national level. I really wanted to have a different experience. I think all the early work we did with Ntosake was the most transformative and helpful for me, over and above the academic piece of "here's how you do organizing."

Ntosake also contributed to the development of Gamaliel's affiliate organizations in South Africa. Mary Gruber and Myrna Nelson were among the women who traveled there periodically to provide training and to support local organizers, congregations, and leaders. One thing they brought with them was Ntosake training. Gruber describes what it was like when she was part of one such visit:

One of the women there had walked most of the way from her village to come to our training. She was the woman who basically got running water for her village through an organizing campaign. I was one of the first of the trainers to do a piece. I started going through what I had planned to say, but then I just froze and I thought, "Oh my God, am I in trouble!"

So I just said what I was thinking. I said, "I think you are all looking at me wondering what this uppity White woman from the middle of the United States is doing here. And she's going to tell us what's what?" I thought that's what they must be thinking. Then I said, "I don't know. I don't know. But we're all women. Many of us are moms or grandmas, sisters, daughters. And maybe that's where we have the connection. And we see things around us that are wrong and not fair and we are feeling compelled to change it, but we don't know how in the heck we're going to do that. And that's what is important to me about this. Maybe that's where we begin. I don't know. But are you willing to go along with me?"

And it totally transformed the whole rest of the day.

For all of the organizing networks, leadership training is a high priority. It is one of the things that distinguishes organizing from the various other ways that people of faith can engage in the public arena. However, getting leaders, especially laity, to take a week to ten days away from home and work, and to pay for the training and the travel, is an ongoing challenge. But when more and more leaders, lay and clergy, receive this high-level professional training, the organizing work back home becomes so much more dynamic and effective.

Leah Wiley is the Director for Training and Development for the DART national organizing network. During her tenure in that role, she has imposed a certain level of discipline that has affected the turnout numbers for national training:

> I brought the tools with me from my six-year stint as an organizer at Faith in Action for Strength Together (FAST) in Pinellas County, Florida. So I started making a series of phone calls with every lead organizer, leading up to a national training, to make sure that they were going to hit their turnout commitments. Training turnout increased significantly with me in this position. And this culture of training and leadership development is *A Thing* in many organizations because of that accountability process that I perfected. I feel like I really push organizers, holding them accountable, and accompanying them in their turnout processes.

Wiley also describes how the nature of DART's national training has changed under her leadership:

> We've gotten more focused on best practices, and sharing stories from local issue campaigns. There were a lot of presentations in our trainings that we eventually deemed unnecessary. The trainings evolve with what's going on, on the ground. For example, we used to do a 10-minute presentation in our research-to-action training on action tickets, on making sure that you give them out to leaders and count them, as a turnout strategy. But it was so unnecessary at the point at which I came into this. We had gotten so much better about how to count turnout and how to leave that up to the local organizations. We didn't need to take up time at our national training to instruct people about how to do their ticket process.
>
> What has taken its place is an hour-long presentation about the self-interest of public officials, and how to deal with the tension that arises when their self-interest is so different from ours. When we walk into a meeting with a sheriff, for example, thinking that what we're proposing is so reasonable that they'll have to agree with us, we are being naïve and we're going to get taken. So, that's just an example of how we've become better at knowing what's going on, on the ground, with our organizations, listening to organizers tell us what their leaders need to hear and learn.

All of that work on Wiley's part is paying off in the form of a new level of seriousness throughout the network regarding the importance of leadership training:

> We are getting better at helping our local affiliates create a culture where leaders go to training, regional and national. Our trainings are where our theology

and our language and our practices really get perfected. We get to hear what's happening in our local affiliates and others get to learn about what worked that can be replicated in other places.

When we have more leaders coming to hear about our best practices, and then implement them back home, that's where the rubber meets the road. It's about leaders making it happen. So if people can come and hear and be inspired, that's significant.

We're helping local organizers get more leaders to training and build it into the culture of the organization. That's just what you do, at the start of every process, is send leaders to regional or national training. Then you implement those learnings when you get back home.

Understanding Issue Work

> I thought about all these men around me who had incredible educations, who'd traveled and seen places. I'd gone to a vocational high school and I'd only traveled downtown! But the advantage I had was that I had been involved in direct action, face-to-face, eyeball to eyeball. I had overcome my fears. I must have done more than 500 actions in a period of four years. I overcame the fears I had with public actions. I was the only one that had that, among all these men I was sitting with. I knew I had my own notches in my belt, around issues and actions.
>
> —Mary Gonzales

Besides fighting for well-deserved roles and opportunities, and bringing greater excellence to network training processes, other changes happen when women assert their insights and gifts into the mix. This is particularly true regarding an organization's approach to issue work. But women insist that, because of their gender, initiating these kinds of changes is an uphill struggle. Pamela Twiss describes one such battle:

> The biggest fight I had was when we first heard Myron Orfield speak at a local clergy event. [Orfield is the director of the Institute on Metropolitan Opportunity at the University of Minnesota.] I remember him talking about how people flush their toilet in suburban Plymouth and money comes out of Minneapolis! It was that whole picture of what metro area disparities looked like and who was paying for what. He gave us a power analysis. I was one of the first people who said that we had to take this up. We had to work on metro inequity issues. It made so much sense to me. We needed a regional approach.
>
> As we were doing more with this in Minnesota, I'd go to these Gamaliel national things and it was clear that people were having all these fights about what was going on in their local communities. But I now understood that those communities couldn't solve their problems on their own. I kept saying that they needed to start thinking about regional work and having Myron Orfield

come and explain the metro inequity analysis. Greg finally said, "Fine. You invite him to the next Gamaliel staff meeting to do a presentation, and we'll see where it goes."

So I got Myron all set up and the day comes for the meeting. Well, his plane is late! When the time came in the meeting to do his presentation, he's not there! And Greg says, "Alright, Pamela. He's not here so you need to explain this to us." So I got up and started explaining it the best I could, but I didn't have any slides or charts ready. I hadn't organized a presentation. Then Myron came after about fifteen minutes of me bumbling around. And he did this presentation and it was very compelling to a lot of people in the room.

But then we got into small groups and started talking about it. And I ended up in a small group where the guys just took my head off about the whole idea and grilled me about where it had been successful. Two of my local [male] colleagues were in that group too and they didn't say anything. They weren't willing to step up and say, "We think this is a good idea, too." They didn't talk about how they were doing this in their Twin Cities affiliates. They just didn't say anything. They were just going to watch me get roasted!

But in the end it became *The Thing* that the whole network did. When Metro Equity became the buzz phrase for the whole network, I made that happen! Before that they weren't paying attention, didn't know about Myron or any of the others working on this. I'm sure that if one of the men had brought it, it would have been received differently. I'm 100 percent sure of that!

Training up a New Generation

In many organizing circles, there is resistance to involving youth to any significant degree in organizing efforts. The arguments vary as to why, from concern about their sometimes volatile or unreliable tendencies to the claim that they don't often have a consistent or large enough base of peers that they will be able to lead or turn out for various actions. However, these attitudes are being challenged more and more these days, as young people dominate in social media and public arena activism, and as their dissatisfaction and anger about the slow pace of cultural and political change grow around issues that directly affect them.

Meghan Sobocienski is one organizer who has always believed that bringing youth into the heart of organizing is a good and fruitful endeavor. In those places where she has organized, her inclusion of young leaders has shifted the dynamics of those organizations in important ways. Here's how she describes her interaction with youth that has led to her success:

While I was at COR [a PICO affiliate in Hayward, California], bringing the voice of young people into the center of the work that involved them—like education work and violence reduction work—became a really important driving force for me. That hadn't been happening much before me. I was told that young people were transient and that institutions were not, so we organize adults and not young people. But I'd also been taught that those closest to the pain need to define the solution! I was pretty proud of getting young people involved.

One campaign was around school closures and the neighborhood middle school in the place where the black and brown kids lived. We were trying to re-open it as a small autonomous community school, a charter. We wanted to keep it open to serve the population that was under threat. We were organizing a lot with parents, which was important. But I'd have parents bringing their kids to meetings and the kids would just sit there. And I was interested in bringing them into the conversation. So I'd start with an activity that would appeal to everyone in the room. Or I'd go to their homes and visit their parents, but I'd spend the first five to ten minutes of my visit getting to know the kids and their interests. I'd put them into small roles at actions at first, but pretty soon I'd get them to share testimonies. Then they became full-fledged leaders.

I find youth to be more willing to fight for things they believe in without having to think all the way through the consequences, and I think that's a good thing. Organizing adults involves a lot of just plain convincing them that what we want is possible. There's less need for that with young people. There's less obedience to the nay-saying voices in society.

Sobocienski's belief and investment in young people in organizing has not only changed the nature of the network organizations she has worked for and the issues they have championed. It has become the cornerstone of the non-profit work she now directs, running youth cooperatives that create jobs for at-risk youth who live in her Southwest Detroit neighborhood.

Leader-Centered Organizing

> Good organizers recognize that we all have the potential to create, but we don't all have the opportunity. So my cause is to provide that opportunity for others to step into that ability to create a world they want to live in.
>
> —eva schulte

Meghan Sobocienski's insistence on involving young people in organizing when the issues directly affect them extends beyond an age-specific popula-tion. Organizations that approach their issue work believing that those closest to the problem get to define the solution center their efforts on leaders who have the most to lose or gain in any given issue, regardless of their age or social status. This concept derives from the term subsidiarity, which comes out of Catholic Social Teaching (part IV of chapter 4 of the *The Compendium of the Social Doctrine of the Church*, 2004).

Mary Lim-Lampe directs a Gamaliel affiliate called Genesis in Oakland, California. She describes the value of the subsidiarity concept, which she began to explore when the organization she directed in Kansas City, Missouri was working on a workforce development campaign:

> I loved creating the narrative that we share out into the world. And I think I brought some guts to the narrative around workforce development. I kept thinking that these White, middle-class neighbors telling about the issue is not as effective as the person experiencing the results of the issue. So I was really adamant that we talk to somebody who would get a job as a result of the program we had won money for. I found this guy who was directly affected and I really stuck with it. After that, the organization started thinking more about developing and elevating people who are directly affected by these issues.

Doran Schrantz learned out of necessity the importance of putting responsibilities squarely on the shoulders of leaders when, as a young organizer, she was preparing to go on maternity leave. This was in the late spring of that year, and the major public meeting they were planning was scheduled to occur in the fall, shortly after she would return from her leave:

> That year my relationship to organizing changed. I had to put a plan in place and line everyone up and get into it with people around their self-interest. There was something very practical and urgent that pushed me into another way of relating to leaders, putting responsibility onto them and grounding it in their self-interest. I felt so good about that! And we did turn out the 1500 people that we said we would, from my two caucuses. I had to have people and myself completely clear by June of that year! It really upped my organizing game. I was going to come back in September and would only have a month before the public meeting.
>
> I was also getting so politicized at that time. I was learning about the corporate conservative movement and their long-term agenda. I was really feeling urgency that we get to another level of relevance as an organization. I saw political operations at work and the mechanisms of power behind them. Then I'd turn around and look at our organization and think, "Oh, we're cute! With our little meetings and little Inreaches!" If we wanted to be relevant through this vehicle, then we had to build something that could compete. There was that drive in me, too.

Mary Gruber was the architect of a leader-centered table of national Gamaliel affiliate presidents, in an effort to put the responsibility for the work of the organization more squarely onto leaders, as opposed to just in the hands of paid organizers. She also believed that creating this leadership table would contribute to the power that the network was building:

I was president of ISAIAH and I wanted to start the Gamaliel Council of Presidents. I saw this Council as a venue for sharing across organizations. I also wanted to level the playing field between the genders and the races of the presidents of organizations. Knowing that many of the presidents were simply figureheads really pissed me off. I was like, we can't be powerful if this continues; if we're going to become a national organization and not just a training institute. There were presidents at that first meeting who had never even been to training! I said, "What?! That's ridiculous!" But they didn't like me, an uppity White lay woman, telling that to powerful White and Black male pastors. But it was the truth!

So anyway, our mission as a Council of Presidents was about how to come together at a national level and create more power. I was interested in how we could accomplish things with not just organizing staff but also presidents working together from the more than twenty states where we had affiliates. We had to create an infrastructure of some sort in order to operate.

Taking on Racial Equity

Faith communities of color have been utilizing the tools and principles of community organizing in the United States at least since the days of the Abolitionists in the mid-1800s. The Civil Rights and Farm Workers movements of the 1960s drew on the Highlander Folk School and organizing traditions of Latin America to train up activists of color, many of whom had deep roots in their faith communities. Some White activists joined as allies in those efforts of communities of color to fight for racial and economic justice, many doing so in response to their religious values.

Despite this rich history of communities of color leading the way in the struggle for justice, many faith-based community organizing networks and affiliates have ongoing internal struggles over racial equity within their own ranks. Women organizing at the local or national levels of the networks are contributing to the breaking down of racial barriers. But the work is difficult and ongoing.

Ana Garcia-Ashley, the only woman and first person of color to serve as executive director of a national organizing network, Gamaliel, describes ways that she is working to shift racial dynamics in her organization:

> In terms of growing the organizers of color pool, because I am a person of color, I have brought more a belief among them that becoming leaders and directors is do-able in this network. I have recruited and encouraged and tried to hold onto and nurture organizers of color.
>
> It's also a goal of mine to have people of color leading in their local affiliates, like Reverends DeNiece and John Welch and Reverend Brisco and Reverend Bigsby and Reverend Marilynn Miller. They are leading in their settings and

seeing that they can make a difference in the world. Staying on top of our African American and immigrant leaders and organizers is important, as well as expanding into the areas where we will find more leaders of color.

One of our funders recently said to me that she didn't realize that Gamaliel was "so Black!" They see us at the center of the work and I claim a little bit of credit for that reality.

The ISAIAH organization in Minnesota where I was active, first as a parish pastor and later as a paid organizer, has struggled throughout its thirty-year history to become more racially diverse. Founded originally by mostly White Catholic and Protestant churches, ISAIAH has had some Latino and African American member congregations. But those communities of color have been in the minority, and ISAIAH's staff and elected leaders for most of its history have been predominantly White, despite numerous attempts over the years to more fully diversify.

In the past ten years, however, ISAIAH's membership and leadership bases have shifted to include significant numbers of leaders and faith communities of color, under the leadership of Executive Director Doran Schrantz. She is a White woman who recognizes that her own racial identity plays a complicating role in their ongoing challenges. But she has overseen the gradual diversification of her organization. She describes in detail how this shifting reality has been intentionally orchestrated, and how it is still very much a work in progress:

Transforming ISAIAH into an organization with leaders of color who are shaping the organization has been one of the hardest things, with the least amount of resolution. This started ten years ago, and even now, almost every day, we realize we've screwed something up in terms of race. There are messes to clean up on a regular basis.

But what happened was, starting back in 2007, I had a set of experiences of feeling really self-critical and critical of ISAIAH. I looked at things we had done and realized how blind we were in terms of race. I had a political revelation that, if we didn't deal with this, we wouldn't be relevant.

There was a set of things in my life that helped influence that: one of my best friends who is a person of color, we confronted these issues in our relationship. A colleague at a partner organization was going through her own path around this question, so I talked to her a lot about it. Our Latino organizing program exploded; totally crashed and burned. Then Terrance Jacob, who had founded Gamaliel's South Africa organizations, came and worked for us. Pastor Paul Slack was coming into the organization at that time. Lisa Amman had gotten into a set of relationships with Black churches in St. Paul while I was on maternity leave. I came back and she had a public meeting at Mt. Olivet, a Black Baptist Church, and I was like, "How did you do that?"

So what we started with was an introduction and training around structural racism and implicit bias. And a lot of training and internal conversations with

White leaders about race. We did this whole house meeting program about race. We talked about it a lot in terms of racial equity in the public arena and we re-did a lot of our issues around how are we impacting things, not just around our good intentions. We took the arenas in which we already worked—like leadership development, relationship building, how we actually operate in public—and asked, "What does it mean to work on an issue campaign with a race lens?"

We had Applied Research Institute do an audit of the organization. We wrote assessments. It was a lot with me, as director. Terrance built some things or modeled them so that people could see how to have Black, Latino, and White people sit with each other and have honest conversations. What does that honest, direct conversation look like and how does it feel and how do you learn not to run away from it when you're feeling totally freaked out or super judged? Recognize that it's normal; keep walking forward. It was like learning a muscle memory of how to live into the discomfort, so that it starts to feel less uncomfortable.

We did a lot of intentional looking at how our issues benefit people of color. We used john powell's stuff about targeted universalism. [powell is the director of the Haas Institute for a Fair and Inclusive Society at the Law School at the University of California, Berkeley.] We got a lot of help and did a lot of trial and error. Then we tended to deep Christian persistence about relating to people and churches of color. We told ourselves that we were going to get turned away, every time, but we were going to keep going back. We never left the table no matter how painful it was or what anyone said. It's never as painful as what people are experiencing in a racist, sexist world! That's what you do when you have faith; you persist. And you learn and grow and persist. And you just believe that at some point you are going to be in relationship in some way.

That attitude, and then the intentional bringing in of staff of color into the mix, and constantly calibrating when people are ready to move into positions of greater import. I knew we couldn't just make someone a director when they didn't yet know how to organize. There are struggles, but over time there was: Terrance's position and power, Pastor Paul's position and power, James Alberts from St. Cloud, Phyllis Hill and the role she played, and now Catalina and Brian. There has been the development of a set of leaders over time and then a communications director and the financial manager who are people of color. Having the chair of our board be a person of color and over half of the members of the board are people of color, people are seeing more and more people of color in roles of prominence.

But there are still also lots of problems, like us being accused of just using people of color. Still, there's more of a culture. We've built some capacity over the last ten years for a more multi-racial culture that can receive and adapt to people coming in and out. It's not as fragile, though it still gets plenty of critique.

Organizers of color admit to having doubts, at times, as to how effective—or not—organizing with faith-based networks and affiliates can be, ultimately, in their journey toward racial justice. Tamisha Walker articulates this ambivalence well. Her testimony also gives voice to a similar struggle for formerly incarcerated people involved in this work:

> People of color are still really trying to make their way in PICO. The organizing model is good. But when you start to incorporate issues of gun violence and mass incarceration; when you start to think about organizing around the pain of the Black community; it's necessary to take the tools and see what's not working. We need to figure out what we can do to refurbish the playbook and examine the context in which we've been organizing.
>
> Now we're often organizing people who aren't largely showing up in congregations. The people we're fighting for at Safe Return aren't centrally located, unless they're in a prison or jail. And we don't need any more street lights or speed bumps! [Issue campaigns sometimes addressed on the neighborhood level.] It's about keeping people from being shot dead in the streets! It's about keeping people from being incarcerated, or from being disenfranchised when they are incarcerated. These are not things that churches are extremely comfortable about getting out there and marching about!
>
> Also, being a woman of color in organizing, a formerly incarcerated one— there aren't many of us—has challenged me to create that space for more formerly incarcerated women to organize in this way.

Walker's final comment speaks to the whole issue of intersectionality, which people with identities that cross gender, class, and race lines must face in this work.

When it comes to racial diversity, most of the organizing that I've been a part of has put me in relationship with African Americans and Latino immigrants. But leaders who identify from other racial or ethnic communities have unique challenges as they make their way in the organizing realm. Mary Lim-Lampe is Chinese American. She tells about how she has helped people change their perception of leaders like her:

> For the most part, you don't see Chinese-American women take charge, take authority. I know I'm changing that for people. I know that I change that for public officials and for people like my colleague's adopted daughter, who is from Korea, who commented to her dad on seeing me as an executive director of an organization. I know I want my own daughter to see me on the stage with a microphone giving instructions to people!

NO BETTER, MORE CHALLENGING TIME THAN NOW

Like congregations and religious denominations, community organizations must continue to evolve and grow if they're going to be powerful vehicles for change for the sake of greater justice. But like any system, those organizations resist change. And like congregations and denominations, sustaining community organizations is extremely challenging. Traditionally, organizing networks and affiliates have depended on individual members and congregations, as well as religious denominations, for significant financial support. With congregations and denominations shrinking in size as well as financial resources, those traditional funding sources are diminishing. Organizations are shifting to greater reliance on foundational grants; but those sources also are challenged, and challenging for organizations to maintain.

Leah Wiley, of DART, speaks for many in the field when she laments:

> There is so much work to do! And not enough money to hire more staff. So I'm the training coordinator, from logistics to agenda to content to presenters. I'm writing the content and preparing the organizers and leaders who present. I'm doing the billing, I'm doing fund-raising. There is so much that needs to be done well.
>
> The nature of a good organizer is to be somewhat of a perfectionist. So I'm often thinking, "I could've done that better!" You have to be open to evaluation, but not to kicking yourself. There's just so much to do and not enough people to do it.

Given all that, faith-based power organizations like DART, Faith in Action, Gamaliel, and the Industrial Areas Foundation are more relevant and needed than ever. People of faith who hold to the concept that "the arc of the moral universe is long, but it bends toward justice"[1] are feeling the strain, in this polarized political and cultural climate, of that arc's extreme length. Nevertheless, we must persist, with all our organizational and collective might, to hasten its bending.

NOTE

1. The quote is first attributed to Unitarian Minister Theodore Parker, derived from a longer passage in his 1853 sermon, "Of Justice and the Conscience," in *Ten Sermons on Religion*, The Collected Works of Theodore Parker, vol. 2, ed. Frances Power Cobbe (London: Trübner and Co., 1879).

Chapter Five

The Transformation
of Communities

"Give to us a possession [of land] among our father's brothers." (Numbers 27:4b)

THE DAUGHTERS OF ZELOPHEHAD: FIVE FEISTY
SISTERS CHALLENGE HEBREW PATRIARCHY

In the Hebrew Scriptures, in the twenty-seventh and thirty-sixth chapters of Numbers, is tucked a remarkable story about the five daughters of Zelophehad. It takes place when the people of Israel are on the verge of moving into the land of Canaan, their "Promised Land." God has commanded Moses to begin dividing up among the tribes and families of Israel the land that they have seen from afar. The patriarchal tradition dictated that this would take place when Moses summoned the male heads of each family to the entrance of the Tent of Meeting, where he and his advisors assembled to do the business of the people.

"Now Zelophehad son of Hepher had no sons, but daughters: and the names of the daughters of Zelophehad were Mahlah, Noah, Hoglah, Milcah, and Tirzah" (26:33).

By the time Moses is doling out land to those who would enter Canaan, Zelophehad has already died. And there is no male heir to represent his family at the Tent of Meeting. Instead, the five daughters of Zelophehad come and stand before Moses, in the presence of all the male heads of households, and make a case for their right to inherit his portion of land. In turn, Moses takes their case to the LORD, who sides with the daughters, commanding Moses to apportion their father's land to them. But the LORD goes even further than either the daughters or Moses have asked. The LORD commands Moses to institute a new ordinance, dictating that from this time forward, whenever a man with only daughters should die, they are to be given his inheritance.

97

Well, some of the men of Israel are upset by this decision to let the daughters of Zelophehad and any future women inherit their fathers' land. They go separately to Moses and his advisors and argue that land given to women could easily be lost to the larger tribe of their father if the daughters choose to marry outside of that tribe. So Moses, under the direction of the LORD, puts a condition on any women who inherit their father's land, that they must marry within their own tribe, or forfeit their father's inheritance.

The daughters of Zelophehad dutifully marry men from their own tribes. But their ordeal isn't over yet, since all of this takes place well before the Israelites actually enter Canaan to take possession of the land. That eventually happens after Moses dies, having been forbidden by the LORD to enter the Promised Land. Once in the land, the daughters of Zelophehad have to present themselves again, this time before Moses' successor Joshua and his advisors, and remind them of the commandment God had made that the daughters be given their father's inheritance.

"So according to the commandment of the LORD Joshua gave them an inheritance among the kinsmen of their father" (Joshua 17:4b).

LARGER CONSEQUENCES

When the daughters of Zelophehad went to Moses demanding that they be given their fair share of the property that the Israelites would possess in the Promised Land, they weren't thinking about changing the overall norms and systems within which their people operated. Their concern was for their own well-being and for the legacy of their father's name in their Hebrew clan. But by their bold initiative, norms and systems were, in fact, changed in ways that would more broadly affect their community and the women who would face similar circumstances in the future. Their story from Numbers is the first time in biblical history when women were allowed to own property.

> I have early life memories of resistance and an understanding of systems. I was very aware that there were "insiders and outsiders" that created "acceptable and unacceptable" people, and that there was power at play within those systems. I was also just aware that you could resist those things and that people could win over those things that were done to people. That was partially because of my dad's experience in Central America, where he learned from powerful activists.
>
> I was raised in a community of my parents' friends who were also activists. Also, my uncle died of AIDS when I was twelve, in 1992, and he was gay. It was the year that RENT came out and there was that narrative and AIDS was very taboo and the LGBT movement hadn't become a big movement yet. So I learned about the brokenness of institutions and how they harm people, and also that we could have power to change those things.
>
> —Meghan Sobocienski

By now it should be understood that changing public policy by winning issue campaigns is not the only or even the primary end goal of faith-based community organizing. Leadership development and the fostering of authentic, powerful community rank as the highest priorities. However, it does *matter* whether or not we're making change happen in our broader communities. It matters a great deal to the women who invest in this work. After all, many of us were attracted to it because of our desire to "make a difference" or even "change the world." Most women in this work also believe that it matters to God that we become agents of change for the sake of greater justice and equity.

WHY NOT JUST HELP PEOPLE?

In the introductory training I do with congregations and leaders that want to get more involved in their communities of context, we often start by imagining together what their other choices are besides community organizing. I might have them take a look at the story of the daughters of Zelophehad, as an example. I tell them to set aside how that story turned out and ask them to suggest what else the faith community around them could have done once the plight of the daughters had been revealed. The discussion often plays out as follows:

> The daughters' neighbors could have taken pity on them and offered to provide food and clothing and other assistance to them, both in the immediate term and after the Israelites arrived in the Promised Land. Or, they could suggest that, since the daughters were not eligible to inherit the land to which their father was entitled, they could be invited to work for another clan member or be trained to provide some other community need for which neighbors would be willing to pay them. Then, perhaps over time, the daughters would earn enough to purchase a small parcel of land upon which they might build a home for themselves. Or, members of the community whose own futures were secure as landowners could have gone to Moses on behalf of the daughters of Zelophehad to ask for an exception or change to the current practice in order to assure the daughters' future well-being.

I name the responses described above as charity, development, and advocacy, respectively. Each approach has its place in the ways that people of faith and religious congregations choose to interact with their neighbors and their broader communities. But we already know how the story of the daughters of Zelophehad actually played out; they organized and spoke up on their own behalf, thereby fostering policy changes that benefitted not only them but all the women like them who would come after. That is the power of community organizing at its best.

I'm reminded of a quote that I often affix to participant folders I provide at trainings. The longer quote draws on an ancient piece of wisdom, sometimes attributed as a Chinese proverb, though evidence for its exact origins is inconclusive. Notably, there is a woman in the succession of those who sometimes get credit for the "Give a man a fish" proverb: nineteenth century novelist Anne Isabella Thacheray Ritchie. In her 1885 novel "Mrs. Dymond" one of her characters says, "If you give a man a fish, he is hungry again in an hour. If you teach him to catch a fish, you do him a good turn" (342). Another popular version of the saying is, "Give a man a fish and you have fed him for a day. Teach a man to fish and you have fed him for a lifetime."

I appreciate a longer quote that borrows from that proverb and fits the context of this discussion. Helpfully as well, it is gender-inclusive in its language. It is attributed to Puerto Rican-born contemporary American activist and artist Ricardo Levins Morales, whose poster of this expanded proverb reads:

> If you give me a fish, you have fed me for a day. If you teach me to fish, then you have fed me until the river is contaminated or the shoreline seized for development. If you teach me to organize, then whatever the challenge, I can join together with my peers and we will fashion our own solutions.

ISSUE CAMPAIGNS

> We have all of these tools for casting our lots together. What would happen if we decided that the kind of disparity between those who have and those who don't—the systemic racism that still endures in this country, the vulnerability of LGBTQ folks, the attacks on women and their rights to their bodies and beyond, equal pay, the Islamophobia, the xenophobia—what if we decided we are all one? And the strategies and the access to relationships and the ways that sectors of our communities each play different parts to being able to build enough power to address that; what if we're willing to say that's what faith calls us to do?
>
> —Stephanie Kolin

I've been a part of several issue campaigns where the outcomes resulted in significant changes to the status quo for members of those communities. My earliest issue work occurred while I was still a parish pastor and relatively new to community organizing. My organizer encouraged me and my church leaders to take on an issue that was very local to where our church was situated. We learned of a proposed "mixed use" housing complex to be built in a nearby suburb where many of our members lived. The developer wanted to build a large complex in which high-end and mid-range market-rate houses and condos would be mixed in with a smaller number of so-called affordable units. We knew that several neighbors near the proposed site objected to the affordable units, claiming that those would attract higher crime rates, and that high housing density would cause difficult traffic congestion. It was your basic Not-in-My-Backyard (NIMBY) argument.

We also knew that the stock of affordable housing in that particular suburb was minimal, and that many low- and middle-income people who already worked in the area couldn't afford to actually live there. Most had a long reverse-commute from the city, with not much to speak of in the way of public transportation. Moreover, most of those workers held the kinds of jobs that any community needs to thrive: school teachers, nursing- and day-care providers, school bus drivers, hairdressers, grocery clerks, and the like.

Our Core Team decided that we would join with those from the community who were in favor of the development as proposed, seeing this as a justice issue as well as a practical matter for the common good. Our organizer set us on a series of steps to equip ourselves for the process. First among them was to do research visits with various parties, including local business owners, workers, the developer of the proposed housing complex, and city council members. We wanted to learn where they stood and whether they could be influenced regarding the matter.

Especially energizing for us was meeting workers and their employers who would benefit the most from the development of the affordable units. For example, we talked with grocery store managers, a school bus dispatcher and her drivers, and local school teachers. We struck gold when we met one particular teacher, a young woman who had grown up in the suburb where the housing complex was to be built. She was a college graduate with a teaching degree who had come back home and landed her first job at the local elementary school. Because of the cost of housing, and her college loan debt, she was living in her parents' basement, with no clear path toward affording her own place in town. She was a great ally and spokesperson for those of us who sought approval for the affordable units.

After doing our research, we began to attend city council meetings, bringing our new allies and as many of our church members as we could, especially those who lived in the suburb in question. Some testified in favor of the developer's proposal while the rest of us cheered or held signs. Some offered accounts of the research we'd done or the stories we'd heard from employers and workers. Some spoke of the assets that such workers contribute and about the absolute necessity for the roles they played in the community.

We also met with our own church council and held forums in the congregation to help our elected leaders and members understand why we were taking a stand on this particular matter. In my preaching, I made reference to the issue and cited biblical underpinnings for our stance. Not surprisingly, we faced a fair bit of opposition from some of our fellow members, who we considered part of the NIMBY crowd. We learned that we weren't as thick-skinned or confident as we thought we were, when people criticized us directly or spoke ill of us and our cause behind our backs.

But eventually the city council voted to approve the housing developers' proposal and the process moved forward with the affordable units included. We had won our first issue campaign! Comments from certain city council members assured us that our particular role in the process had been influential. We also learned some important lessons and further developed as leaders, both in our congregation and in the public arena. We learned that there is a formal "organizing cycle" to be followed when taking on an issue. We realized in hindsight that, if we had paid closer attention to the full set of strategies in that cycle, we might have encountered less opposition and positioned ourselves for greater advantage in subsequent issues we might want to tackle.

THE ORGANIZING CYCLE

My first issue campaign in 2005 was for affordable housing in Pinellas County, Florida. Through my work with the leaders there we got the county to establish an affordable housing trust fund. They put $10,000,000 in the first year, $5,000,000 the next. Over the time that I was there, it got funded with $20,000,000! And, we got to count how many affordable units got built or rehabbed. I think it was around 3500 in my time there, because of the trust fund that we moved through into reality.

It was such a fun campaign because it had results all across the county, and we knew people who were moving into that housing. Working with the leaders was so much fun, and interfacing with the county commission, and preparing leaders to make their testimony, and packing the county commission meetings.

That was my entrée into organizing. That trust fund is still in operation. I think it has like $100,000,000 in it now! When I hear the organizers there update us on that process, I get a little twinge of excitement and pride, that I got to help start that.

—Leah Wiley

When aiming to create change around any given issue, those involved in faith-based organizing typically follow a clear path, or cycle, to get there. Depending on the scope and complexity of the issue, the organizing cycle can take anywhere from a few months to a year or more to complete. All along the way, the priorities of building relationships and identifying and developing leaders remain constant, regardless of whether or not the process delivers an ultimate win of systemic change.

Various versions of the organizing cycle exist and are employed by different organizing groups, but all have the same basic components, prioritized in this clock-wise order:

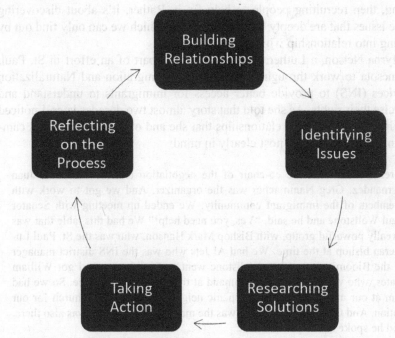

Figure 5.1. The Organizing Cycle

Building Relationships

In building relationships, there are particular types of them to pursue: with congregational members, with neighbors and other community stake-holders, with decision-makers, with other organizations with whom the community organizing group wants to interact. In each relationship-building effort, multiple purposes are at play: deepening a sense of community and common cause; learning what people really care about and would be willing to fight for; discovering who has the ability to contribute to or hinder the change we're seeking; building our collective determination and power in order to catalyze that change.

Relationship building, in the organizing realm, starts with deep listening. I described this kind of listening in the first and second chapters, when leaders go one-on-one with other members of their congregations and communities, to really get to know them and what makes them "tick." Listening also happens at house meetings that leaders host, to learn what issues people really care about and would be willing to work on in order to create change. Choosing issues in this realm isn't just about looking around to see what needs fixing, then recruiting people to help fix it. Rather, it's about discovering those issues that are deeply in people's hearts, which we can only find out by getting into relationship with them.

Myrna Nelson, a Lutheran lay woman, was part of an effort in St. Paul, Minnesota to work through what was then Immigration and Naturalization Services (INS) to provide better access for immigrants to understand and exercise their rights. As she told that story almost two decades later, I noticed that it was the range of relationships that she and others forged in that campaign that she still held most clearly in mind:

> I remember I was the co-chair of the negotiation team, with Pastor Juan Fernandez. Greg Nammacher was the organizer. And we got to work with members of the immigrant community. We ended up meeting with Senator Paul Wellstone and he said, "Yes, you need help!" We had this table that was a really powerful group, with Bishop Mark Hanson, who was the St. Paul Lutheran bishop at the time. We had Al Jets who was the INS district manager in the Bloomington office. Wellstone went to Washington and got William Gates, who was like third in command at the national INS office. So we had him at our meeting, and 350 Hispanic neighbors were in the church for our action. And Chris Coleman, who was the mayor in St. Paul, he was also there, and he spoke at our public event.

Identifying Issues and Researching Solutions

Tamisha Walker was drawn into organizing when she was hired by a PICO (now Faith in Action) affiliate in Richmond, California while they were in the issue-identification and research phases of an organizing cycle:

> This PICO group was looking for formerly incarcerated folks who had a felony to become part of a research team. They hired nine of us formerly incarcerated. The idea was that there were a lot of tables talking about re-entry and the formerly incarcerated coming back into communities, but they didn't have any directly impacted people at the table creating those plans. So they put this team together to build a re-entry plan from the perspective of our experience.
>
> We did participatory research of over 190 formerly incarcerated people. We came up with four top areas of concern: jobs, housing, childcare, and family

reunification. Then we developed a report on the conditions of the formerly incarcerated and presented it to the community and members of our local government.

When identifying issues and researching solutions, we apply a set of criteria to help determine whether or not the change we want to create around any given effort we pursue is achievable.

1. *Distinguish Between Problems and Issues*

We need to take a fairly large or chronic problem and cut it down to the size of an issue that we can manage, given the capacity of our organization. For example, we probably can't solve the problem of hunger in our whole metropolitan region. But we can work on the issue of bringing a well-supplied grocery store into a particular neighborhood that is considered a food desert.

Through her leadership in a campaign with ISAIAH of Minnesota, Mary Gruber and her compatriots had to wrestle with how to cut a set of huge, interrelated problems in her community into a specific issue they could take on to begin to address them. In the process, they also had to decide not to settle for too small of a response to their concerns:

> I remember going to our neighborhood public school with my core team, to meet with teachers and administrators. We learned that they spent the first six weeks of school looking for shoes, and mattresses for kids to sleep on! It would have been really easy to just have a shoe drive. But I didn't want to do that. I kept asking, "Why don't these kids have shoes and beds?"
>
> We could see that decision-making that affected the school district was much bigger than just the school board, that it had to do with our economy, the Met Council, the State Legislature, etc. That's when we met Myron Orfield and we had all the analysis of the neighborhoods within the cities.
>
> My kids were going to school in one of the most difficult parts of St. Paul. But we were learning about the root causes and I did not want to do a shoe drive! I was very interested in doing work around creating jobs that paid living wages. That would affect housing, education, transportation. They all affect each other.
>
> We decided to work on removing the barriers for polluted sites to be cleaned up for business development opportunities, so that we could have more living wage jobs in St. Paul.

2. *Choose What Resonates*

We need to know that there is heartfelt investment in the issue among the people we're working with. That's why we start by having conversations with those closest to us as well as with those most closely impacted by any given issue. And we're going to need strength in numbers—people standing with us who are determined to win because they have a real stake in the outcome.

Maureen Geddes, a Catholic lay woman, was working for ISAIAH, organizing in the Minneapolis suburb of Richfield in the late 1990s, when she and her leaders decided to find out what was on the hearts and minds of the neighbors who lived near their churches:

> We did an outreach into the neighborhoods in Richfield on two weekends in October; nice weekends, people out raking, etc. We invited all the parishes, whether or not they were members of our organization. We had a ten-minute-long script. We were looking for concerns for the neighborhood.
>
> We knocked on 3,000 doors and then we went and reported the results to the city council. As a result, we could enter into the brewing conversation about the new runway being proposed for the nearby airport. People were getting the runaround in terms of who they could influence.
>
> Well, we ended up getting the Federal Aviation Administration people from Washington to a meeting, and our representative from the Eighth District, who was so into transportation, and the president of Delta. We had this big round table and our leaders talked to them.
>
> Afterwards the congressman said, "This was fantastic! We've never had them all in the same room, where they can't just pass the buck!" People in the community got a sense of the power they could actually wield on important matters.

3. Analyze What's Possible

We need to understand the current political or cultural climate and whether there's a good chance that, given that climate, we can win on the issue. That's why we do concrete research, have conversations with those who are in decision-making positions regarding their take on the issue, and determine what's possible given the current realities.

Meghan Sobocienski directs Grace in Action Collectives, a set of youth- and worker-owned businesses in her Southwest Detroit neighborhood that were created and still operate within a community organizing framework. The Collectives partner with Grace in Action faith community where her husband, John Cummings, is the pastor. Sobocienski describes how she and her leaders recognized and took advantage of the growing trends and opportunities of the culture to address some of the needs in their community:

> We were hearing people in our community and our congregation say they couldn't come to church because they were working on their own economic sustainability by doing other work apart from their day jobs. So I brought people together to create some vision, to consider what they might do together to solve some of the ground-level problems.

We had a growing tech industry around us that was making lots of money around things like phone apps and Angry Birds. We brought young people together into what became Radical Productions, a youth-run technology collective that does community-based graphic design, coding, and app development.

We kept listening and building together with people on a high level and a low level. The high level was with people who were already powerful, like lawyers and business consultants. We started to look for people who could join the board, like someone who is influential at the public school level.

But we were also strategizing with people on the ground: women who had the ability to sew and clean, who eventually formed a cleaning cooperative; and youth who were artistic and technically savvy for programing, who formed Radical Productions and Stitching up Detroit, our screen printing cooperative. They're all making a decent living now, in these various businesses that they run.

4. Articulate Solutions

We need to determine what our demands will be that, if met, will give us the outcomes we desire. This is another place where research comes into play, as we learn what solutions have been found to similar concerns elsewhere. But we can also use our imaginations, envisioning what we believe to be possible and just, given the unique context we are addressing.

While I was an ISAIAH organizer we joined a coalition of organizations that was working to pass a Living Wage Ordinance in Minneapolis. We had a concrete set of demands that we developed, many of which we borrowed from similar campaigns in other cities where this had been effective, and some of which we fashioned to fit our particular setting. The demands were that any company of a certain size that was either managing city contracts for services or receiving tax incentives to develop or build in the city would be required to pay a certain significant percentage of their workforce a living wage. That wage had been determined based on a formula showing how much the head of a working family would need to earn in order to support their household and stay above the federal poverty level.

5. Locate a Focal Point

We need to identify a person in charge or an authoritative body that can deliver on the set of specific demands we present, within a specific period of time. This is the person or entity that we will focus our attention and actions on as we move to create the change we want to see.

For our Living Wage Campaign, our focal points were the mayor of Minneapolis and the City Council. All of the pressure we brought to bear on the effort we focused on those two centers of power. They held the authority to contract out various city services and grant tax incentives to companies who wanted to do business in Minneapolis. They alone would have the ability to withhold contracts and incentives from those who did not meet the criteria of the proposed Living Wage ordinance. We persuaded them to pass the measure by meeting with them individually, by showing up with numbers and testimonies at their meetings, by hosting a series of town hall forums in each of their wards, by writing letters to the editor of the local paper, and by negotiating the exact terms of the ordinance with them and their administrative staffs, until we had agreement from enough of them to pass it.

6. Determine Clear Outcomes

We need to be able to measure whether a win on the issue will lead to actual improvements in the lives of those impacted by the change. Otherwise, the win will feel shallow and discouraging, both to those who worked hard to gain it as well as to others who had hoped to benefit from the effort. Measurable wins help us track progress as new efforts toward the desired change are implemented; and they put us in a strong position for the next challenge we decide to take on together.

Mary Gruber tells a remarkable story about the measurability of the Brownfields Campaign's outcomes, and how she got to share those measurable results with a national figure:

In Gamaliel's early National Leadership Assembly (NLA) days, there was a delegation going to Washington, D.C., and they had a meeting set up with Al Gore, who was Vice President in the second term. Our job in the meeting with Gore was to ask him to be a keynoter at our next NLA. Why not ask?

Somehow he had become aware of the work we were doing in St. Paul. He had actually said my name in a speech prior to that, at some institute think tank. His interest was the part about cleaning up the pollution. Our interest was the jobs. He found out about our work and he talked about it and he named me, a nurse, with four kids, all that. He said in that speech, "Look at the work Mary is doing with her church and other churches to get this to happen!"

So we're all waiting to meet with him in D.C. He comes in, we all stood up and he shook everyone's hand. Then we sat down and had our meeting. When it was my turn to talk, I was right across the table from Gore. I started in on my piece and he interrupted me and said, "Wait a minute, Mary: 'Turn polluted dirt into pay dirt,' right?" It was out of left field. But I said, "Yes sir, that is so right!" And he goes, "How's that going?"

I had just checked with the state about where we were at with the number of jobs, so it was on the tip of my tongue. I said, "I'm so glad you asked. I just learned where we're at. We've saved more than 3,000 jobs that pay living wages. And we've already created 10,000 more." He said, "Oh, that's fantastic!" Everyone else in the room is pretty impressed, too.

So after the meeting, he gets up and he walks all the way around this big table, right up to me, and says, "Mary, let's talk a little more about that." I never would have had that opportunity in a million years had it not been for the work we were doing here. It was note-worthy and there was recognition.

Taking Action

Once we've identified our issue and done our research, we're ready to take action. It's likely that action will come in multiple forms. Each action is intended to call greater public attention to the issue, to build support and influence, and to get us closer to the decision-makers we've identified, applying whatever pressure is needed to get them to make the right decision.

Here's where our relationship work comes back into play, as we reconnect with people we've met and work to turn them out for the actions that we take. Depending on the issue, and the decision-maker or decision-making body in focus, our action might come in the form of people testifying or demonstrating at a council or board meeting or attending a public hearing. Or the action might be in the form of mobilizing leaders to show up with a clever message to decision-makers.

A few paragraphs back, Mary Gruber introduced us to ISAIAH of Minnesota's issue work they called their "Brownfields Campaign." Myrna Nelson also was a leader in that effort. She continues the description, providing additional detail:

> We had started out thinking about job creation and how could we attract businesses to the east side of St. Paul. We were working with the St. Paul Port Authority and a woman there told us that they had a lot of businesses that wanted to come to St. Paul that couldn't find suitable land. But then there were sites that were what they called "brown sites." So like, where a gas station had been but when they left they didn't have to clean it up. And there were federal Super Funds that were available to clean up polluted sites.
>
> If we could get our state legislature to acquire some of those funds to clean up these polluted lands, we could get businesses in St. Paul. We did interviews and research and cold-calling to other places in the state asking if they had these kinds of things. Then we went to the House, the Senate, and the Governor on this issue and none of them had it on their agendas.

In order to get the attention of these important lawmakers, ISAIAH leaders came up with an action they called "Turning Polluted Dirt into Pay Dirt," the phrase that Al Gore remembered later in the meeting with Mary Gruber. The action was to bring hundreds of ISAIAH leaders to the capitol on a given day, when lawmakers were in session and the governor was in town, and deliver onto each one's desk a small plastic bag of dirt. In the bag with the dirt was a note card with the "pay dirt" campaign slogan, a description of the problem, the proposed solution, and the demand that they put the issue on their current legislative agenda.

I was at the press conference ISAIAH held on the capitol steps that day, where a dump-truck they had rented pulled up and deposited at our feet the hundreds of bags of dirt. I took part in delivering those bags of dirt to our senators' and representatives' offices and I remember the amused looks we got from their legislative assistants. Myrna Nelson recalls what happened after that and a series of other actions:

> By the time the legislative session was over, they had allocated $60,000,000 for the clean-up of Brownfields! So if you look over on the east side by Phalen Corridor, where all the Health Partners offices are, that's all because of our Brownfields legislation. That was an exciting campaign!

Often the most effective and ultimate action comes in the form of a public meeting that the organization hosts, at which all the various parties related to the issue come together. Public meetings can be relatively contained, on the order of town hall forums. Or they can be impressively large, on the order of thousands of participants gathered in a huge sanctuary or event arena.

At a public meeting, well-prepared leaders fill specific rehearsed roles. There will be those who chair the meeting, those who give testimony, those who present our demands to decision-makers, those who pray, those who sing, and the invested audience ready to voice their support for the issue, or their disappointment if decision-makers are reticent. Those we have identified as who can deliver on our demands will have been invited and informed in advance as to what our demands will be, so that they can prepare for how they will respond publicly. We'll work diligently to gain the attendance of those decision-makers, impressing upon them how it will be in their best interest to participate and cooperate. We will have invited the press and all our allies—individuals and organizations—who have a stake in the outcome of the issue.

Let's go back to Myrna Nelson's earlier account of the effort she was a part of regarding the INS and immigrants' access to key resources. Nelson picks up here by describing the large public meeting that was a turning point in that campaign. In this case, while the public was gathering in a large sanctuary, singing and hearing immigrants' stories, a smaller team of leaders was in an adjacent room meeting with INS and other government officials:

> Pastor Juan and I were the co-chairs of the negotiation team. We had nine demands and I remember they were things like having a Spanish speaking person at the INS office, having the office open one night during the week from 6–9, having a phone available in detention centers so that people could speak with

their family members who were detained, having required papers available in libraries, those sorts of things. It was simple things; it was about treating people civilly! What was happening was the backlog for citizenship papers was so bad, by the time you qualified in one area and were working on the other area, the first had lapsed.

So anyway, we negotiated and we were shocked to get so many yeses! The methodology we used was brilliant. (I'm not saying I was particularly brilliant, but I *was* part of the team.) We used a lot of imagination and strategies. We were so surprised when we got agreements instead of arguments, we almost didn't know what to do!

Afterward we all paraded out into the sanctuary where the hundreds of people were and announced our results and were applauded and cheered and there were speeches and singing and celebration.

Reflecting on the Process

Once we've concluded our action phase of the organizing cycle, we will spend significant time and effort reflecting on the entire process. Besides hopefully winning on our issue, a high priority is learning from our efforts. Reflection usually starts with an evaluation immediately following an action. Key leaders stay after the official event ends as an organizer walks us through the agenda, asking for honest feedback for each of those who had roles and for the effort as a whole. This is the time when we analyze how we did with our turnout work, how each presenter's piece went, how well the chairs managed the time and the tone, whether we got what we wanted from our decision-makers, what we could have done to have a more effective action. We celebrate where we did well; we point out where we fell short. We praise those who stepped up into new leadership roles. We work to get at what happened for those who were less effective.

This opportunity to elevate and then evaluate with leaders in itself can be transformational. Louisa Fletcher-Pacheco recalls how this was true for one of the leaders she worked with:

> During one of our issue campaigns I met this woman named Teresa. She came from one of the high rises that got involved in our campaign. I challenged her to speak publicly at the Environmental Commission public hearing to weigh the community's input on the placement of the filtration plant. I also asked her to bring her community out for this hearing because: power in numbers.
>
> She had never done this before. But I prepped her and when she went to the mic she commanded the room. And when she walked away she held up a sign that said NO FILTRATION PLANT IN THE BRONX. The whole crowd in the auditorium broke into applause and chants. She was ten feet tall that day!
>
> Several years after I left the Bronx, I met up with Teresa again and she had become the president of her local organizing affiliate. She told me that cam-

paign and that action made her realize her own voice and power. It made her believe in herself again. It turned out that, up to that point she had been in an abusive relationship. But after that she left the man who had been oppressing her. I feel like that story is truly what organizing is about.

The reflection phase continues beyond the immediate evaluation session at the end of the action. Because this is faith-based community organizing, often we hold some kind of service or ritual to ground our process in our faith traditions. If we've been successful in gaining a win on our issue, the service will be mostly celebratory in tone. If our outcomes are ambiguous or worse—we didn't win—then our service will likely have elements of lament and contemplation. Such ritual gatherings will be attended by those who worked so hard, sometimes for many months, to get us to where we are at that point. But especially if there's been a win following our actions, we also invite those who helped us get there, including key allies and any decision-makers upon whom we were putting the pressure to deliver on our demands. Community-building is an intentional outcome of all of our hard work. Faith-oriented gatherings, when authentic and inclusive, help build community.

The reflection period sometimes includes closely tracking that the agreed-upon steps are taken to implement the changes we've won in our action. Holding people accountable to the commitments they've made is essential. Karen Brau learned some difficult truths about this while working on a housing issue in the Baltimore neighborhood where she was a pastor:

> I learned a lot about city and regional planning and also that, when you get a law passed, if no one is watching closely, the law isn't followed! We got some statutes on the books and then people would find ways around them. It's about learning how much it takes to have democracy with any kind of democratic tendencies at all, in terms of people's accountability. It's a lot of effort.

Meghan Sobocienski remembers how efforts she was a part of during her time as a young organizer in California continued well beyond the point at which they won their issue campaign:

> We worked on bringing in this violence reduction campaign to our community and we won a big pile of money for that. It was a parcel tax that got us the money. This was a version of Ceasefire, similar to the Boston model. Then I got to lead the implementation process with a set of leaders. I was pretty terrified! It was about making sure the program was implemented in the ways the legislature and the community wanted it.
> I didn't want to screw up the several million dollars of implementation funding. We stayed at the table with the city to make sure the right consultants were

hired and that we were at the decision-making tables. It was part of my job to make sure that church and community leaders, not just staff people, were a part of that process.

Reflecting on how we conduct issue campaigns should be instructive in the long-term, as organizers and leaders consider what they might do differently in the future, given what they learned from this effort. Ana Garcia-Ashley describes an issue campaign she led early in her organizing career that, although it was successful, had its "messy" components:

> We took on a porn shop in a neighborhood. You had a neighborhood that was lower-to-middle income. We were fighting to get a grocery store there. In the meantime, there's this thriving porn business going on, with people coming from not that area to do business there.
> So we started a campaign to shut it down. It doesn't belong here. These people aren't from here. We started taking photos to intimidate the clients. We found out where the owner was in a very affluent community and we went after him. We put flyers out and let all his neighbors know. He called it defamation of character, invasion of his family and privacy, that his family was damaged. But we said he was damaging our families! They ended up having to shut down because of our work.
> It was my first conflict and it was messy. I learned that we couldn't be as reckless as we had been; that we needed to be more sophisticated. When we would fight slum lords and landlords, we learned to get help from other resources, like the university, from politicians, and building more allies, instead of just going with our leaders and our picket signs. If it hadn't been for the really good bishop we had, who was running interference for us, we could have been in big trouble.

ORGANIZING BEYOND
NATIONAL NETWORK AFFILIATES

Most of the issue campaigns that I have used to illustrate the points of this chapter happened within the context of community organizing affiliates of the various national networks. I advocate strongly for leaders and communities of faith to join with such organizations. Those networks and affiliates have proven track records of impactful organizing and power-building. Their training programs are well-established and first-rate. They employ professional staff with experience in issue work and leadership development. And their reputations with funders is significant and essential.

However, for a variety of reasons, congregations and their leaders might choose to branch out in other directions than network and affiliate organizing. Meghan Sobocienski was a PICO organizer for several years, but now does significant organizing work in her Southwest Detroit neighborhood that is not connected to any organizing affiliate. In partnership with other community groups and allies, what Meghan and her leaders have accomplished, and the plans they have for future development, are worth noting:

> When Radical Productions started, we didn't have a lot of experience at the table. The kids wanted to generate money, ala Angry Birds. They started by building websites for people. But it was assembly-line work. They were simply responding to what the clients wanted to see, rather than tapping into their own creativity. And they weren't generating significant revenue.
>
> So we took a step back and listened again. We wrote a grant to develop a curriculum that would turn the participants from being client-focused to community-focused. We worked with the Detroit Future Schools; that included mentors and young people. It was a participatory design process of eight people who developed the curriculum. It was essentially the organizing cycle. They'd listen in neighborhoods and ask the big questions about what people were concerned about.
>
> What kept coming up was the problem with air quality and all the trucks that were stopping and idling in the neighborhood. We did a ton of research and met with our state representative, the director of the Southwest Detroit Community Benefits Coalition, the director of the U.S. Health Department, the director of the Clean Air Project, and with youth in nearby Dearborn that were doing similar things. We met with Data Driven Detroit and with Microsoft.
>
> We gained some new mentors and got some funding to cut some issues. The first one was a trial starter app, American Truck Idle, that allows residents to video idling trucks in violation of the city's statutes about idling. Then we could track the impact of exhaust on the air quality in the neighborhood.
>
> The next thing we want to do is to work with Data Driven to make the air quality sensors be trackable and map-able, in order to track the pollution coming from factories in the area. The government is tracking those things, but people in the neighborhoods don't trust those reports. We're hoping to be able to access those sensors with our app, so we can determine whether the reports are accurate.
>
> We're also connecting with area organizations that want to confront those who are polluting or not reporting on the pollution. These young people are the ones providing the digital tool that gives those organizers what they need to do their issue work around the problems.
>
> 100% of the people we listened to, and the very young people themselves, have asthma in their families, certainly in part because of the poor air quality. Now those young people are being paid for the research they're doing for this issue work.

Susan Leslie describes how some Unitarian Universalist congregations have ventured beyond organizing within network affiliate structures:

> Nowadays there's a whole 'nother level of organizing going on that some of our congregations are a part of. The difference is that it's front-line communi-

ties doing the organizing and then looking for allies in the faith communities. Congregations take direction from the very people most impacted by the issues.

In Arizona, back in 2010, when things were getting so bad there around immigration after the introduction of the SB1070 bill, there was a grass-roots group called Puente that was organizing the migrant community in the barrios and they were looking for allies. Some of our congregations started doing solidarity work with them. We had our "Standing on the Side of Love" campaign and we had folks out there in their yellow "Love" t-shirts and their banners. It was a really big campaign that drew a lot of people.

We also had our General Assembly in 2012 focused solely on justice. We had the event scheduled to happen in Phoenix. But there had been a boycott called for in Arizona after they passed SB1070. The UUA had already signed on the dotted line for our General Assembly. We would have been out $600,000 at the hotel! People were starting to have fights about going vs. not going and boycotting.

I talked to the organizers of Puente and told them about the fights and asked them what we should do. And they said, "Well, you're not breaking the boycott if you come in at our invitation. If you're willing to have the Assembly be all about justice and working together with us and other groups, we'll invite you in."

People dropped their objections to coming into Arizona because we'd been invited by the grass-roots folks who wanted our alliance. We ended up having a huge public action down at tent city and we had all kinds of faith-based and grass-roots organizers from around the country doing workshops. It was a chance to really just get more people who were interested in doing social justice.

HOPE IN THE MIDST OF STRUGGLE

I find all these stories about people and communities of faith fostering systemic, sometimes lasting change, exciting and inspiring. I have experienced and witnessed profound moral and spiritual meaning for people engaged in this work, and genuine improvement in the lives of those impacted by these efforts. As daunting as the political and cultural challenges are, the tools and principles of faith-based community organizing stand the test of time, bringing hope and results where despair and stagnation have held sway. I resonate with these words of Rabbi Stephanie Kolin as I bring this chapter to its conclusion:

Organizing for me just gives me hope. I didn't understand before, that the connections between people were the things that were going to save us. That were going to reveal God in the world. That were going to mean that people didn't need to be isolated in their hopelessness or alone in their brokenness or afraid in their pain; whether that pain was not having enough or being vulnerable because they're a certain kind of person with a certain kind of identity, whether race or sexuality or poverty or any of the things that make us us. We're so alone until the rest of the world is willing to see us and feel that our destiny is aligned, that our lots are cast together, that I have a claim on your life and you have a claim on mine.

What I started to get, when I came into organizing was, "Oh crap! That's a lot of work!" To build those relationships and that trust and unearth the stories that drive us and to understand the stories that drive people that don't look like us. And to then say, "Alright, what are we going to do about the pain in the world? Are we just going to mourn it? Pray about it? Or could we actually weave together these relationships, build the power we need to actually make lasting change in the world and make sure that the word strategy is a holy word?" Because if we're strategic enough, we can actually make the change that will heal pain and have measurable impact in the world.

Chapter Six

Women's Paths to Power

> With Jesus were some women who had been cured of evil spirits and infirmities, [including] Mary, called Magdalene, from whom seven demons had gone out. (Luke 8:2)

MARY MAGDALENE: APOSTLE TO THE APOSTLES

Throughout the New Testament Gospel accounts of Jesus' life, a number of women play noteworthy roles. Two named Mary receive the most attention, the first being Jesus' mother. Mary Magdalene is the second of the two, about whom much ancient as well as contemporary speculation has been generated. Very few facts are known about Mary Magdalene, and much of what has been touted about her has little evidential support; namely the poorly made assumption throughout much of history that she was a prostitute. The most we know of her past is that she had been seven-times demon-possessed, and that it was likely Jesus who drove those demons out, contributing to her devotion to him.

Mary Magdalene's role in the Jesus narrative is central, as indicated by the frequent mention of her presence as one of his closest companions, and by the fact that she was the first to witness the resurrected Jesus and tell the other disciples of his rising. The latter is what has earned her the title Apostle to the Apostles. (The original meaning of the word apostle is messenger.) This Mary's prominence raises interest and speculation in part because people can't help but be curious about her past and how it, along with other factors, led her into such a powerful position alongside Jesus.

HOW THEY GOT THERE

Each of the women I interviewed for this book has her own personal back story about what led her to become so dedicated to the work of faith-based community organizing, and influential in various realms through her engagement with the field. It's instructive to learn that there is not just one "type" of woman who is attracted to this arena, nor one particular path by which women come to the work. As we explore the backgrounds and motivations that compelled these women into this field, we might recognize something of ourselves or others around us. Perhaps there are people—women or men— who might venture onto a path toward community organizing more readily, knowing that others like them have been on similar journeys.

Throughout biblical history, women's lives—like that of Mary Magdalene— took new and more fruitful turns, due in part to their past struggles or the quests they were on all along the way. Each brought her past experiences and personal aspirations into life-altering encounters or situations that set her on a new way forward. These ancient women's stories prefigure the experiences of the contemporary women whom we have come to know in these pages. I call some of these biblical figures briefly to mind, from my own tradition's sacred texts, as we explore more fully the paths to power of our contemporary examples.

It's in Her Nature

At that time Deborah, a prophetess, wife of Lappidoth, was judging Israel. She used to sit under the palm of Deborah between Ramah and Bethel in the hill country of Ephraim; and the Israelites came up to her for judgment. She sent and summoned Barak son of Abinoam from Kedesh in Naphtali, and said to him, "The Lord, the God of Israel, commands you, 'Go, take position at Mount Tabor, bringing ten thousand from the tribe of Naphtali and the tribe of Zebulun. I will draw out Sisera, the general of Jabin's army, to meet you by the Wadi Kishon with his chariots and his troops; and I will give him into your hand.'" Barak said to her, "If you will go with me, I will go; but if you will not go with me, I will not go." And she said, "I will surely go with you." (Judges 4:4–9a)

Although this book is about transformation, some of the women featured came upon organizing as part of a very natural progression in their development. In other words, they didn't have to change much to embrace organizing. The tools and principles of the field simply equipped them to become better at what they already were inclined to do. Here, in excerpts from my interviews, three of these women recall similarly how their involvement with organizing meshed with a way of being that had been evident in them for a long time.

> I have been organizing since I was in the third grade, by nature. My third-grade teacher told my parents that I was a field general on the playground. As a girl, that was not a good thing in the south in the early '60s! But I wanted a team and I wanted to put it together myself, and place them in their positions based on their talents. And I wanted to coach them.
>
> —Emily Eastwood

> I was doing organizing before I knew what it was. From childhood, different leadership opportunities would come to me, whether it was student council or things like that. Faith has always been key for the whole process. I didn't always call myself a faith organizer. I didn't even use the term "organizing." I was just doing what needed to be done.
>
> —Onleilove Alston

> My mom says I've always been a connector, to connect people and build community, to create spaces of belonging. Ever since I was little. So there's a natural relationality to who I am. Organizing was so many things coming together for me. It resonated with my soul and my way of being. It taught me to look at the connection between the individual and the systemic.
>
> —Melissa Reed

It Runs in the Family

> I am reminded of your sincere faith, a faith that lived first in your grandmother Lois and your mother Eunice and now, I am sure, lives in you. (2 Timothy 1:5)

Families of origin and the primary people with whom they were in relationship growing up played an important part in how some women developed the values and attitudes that led them into organizing. For four of the women I interviewed, this was especially true.

> My family, during WWII, had sponsored a young man who was Japanese, from one of the internment camps. And he came to live with us and was able to go to school. Eventually his whole family came and was able to settle in the area. It was not a very popular thing to do, to have somebody like that in the neighborhood. But my parents did that.
>
> —Maureen Geddes

My grandmother was very poor and isolated in a country town in the Dominican Republic. There was a struggle for electricity and there wasn't always water. There were limited resources, but she inspired me to be an organizer, to be a fighter, to be a person of faith, to take on powers and principalities. It was just her spirit. She was actively involved in controlling her own environment.

My grandmother got really sick and tired of those trucks, from the U.S. corporations that had come to our region to harvest the sugar cane and pineapples, going back and forth in front of our houses on the dirt roads. She had me running around knocking on doors and getting people to come to a protest that she was organizing. The next morning, she lined everyone up and blocked the road. I remember seeing all these people with this barefooted, tall, dark woman with two braids standing there, and seeing these machines just stopped!

Eventually what happened was that they put these speed bumps in the road, which is what she wanted, to slow down the trucks. She had asked for those for a long time, but never got it until she organized that blockade. There was no way to stop their use of the road, but she was at least able to slow them down.

—Ana Garcia-Ashley

I grew up going to protests with my parents. I remember when the Detroit Free Press was on strike because they weren't paying workers well. So we stopped getting the paper. And we always had to buy American cars because my grandparents were part of the union. Still today my parents have an American car, because of the union workers.

My grandma was an organizer for the union, one of the first women organizers for AFSME in Detroit. There's that piece that's like legacy for me.

My dad was always fighting for things. When I was eight, he went to Central America with the Center for Global Education and came back and was very much a different person—very aware of and passionate about what had happened and what the U.S. had done in giving weapons to the government to kill innocent people, and what happened in the 80s in Guatemala and El Salvador. I think I really listened to a lot of it.

—Meghan Sobocienski

My grandfather had been in the Bread and Roses strike. Laurence was a mill town—where we lived. When my grandfather was twelve, his job was to keep the workers they called "scabs" from getting out of the river after they had been thrown in, so they couldn't come back and take the jobs. I grew up with these stories.

My grandfather became a union activist in the mills. That's what he did his whole life. I had another grandfather who was an anarchist. My family had this working-class union activist ethos.

My parents jumped the border, with the GI Bill, into the suburbs in New Hampshire, and started building a Democratic party where there hadn't been one before. Because they were there on the ground floor, as a kid I met all the Dems who ran for president! I had U.S. senators in my home; the governor, when we managed to elect a Democrat.

I'm a third grader and there's a U.S. senator in my living room and I'm having to give a speech in class the next day, and I asked him if he gets nervous when he speaks to groups! So it was really in my blood. I leafleted from the time I was five.

—Susan Leslie

A Way of Faithful Living

Now in Joppa there was a disciple whose name was Tabitha, which in Greek is Dorcas. She was devoted to good works and acts of charity. At that time she became ill and died. When they had washed her, they laid her in a room upstairs. Since Lydda was near Joppa, the disciples, who heard that Peter was there, sent two men to him with the request, "Please come to us without delay." So Peter got up and went with them; and when he arrived, they took him to the room upstairs. All the widows stood beside him, weeping and showing tunics and other clothing that Dorcas had made while she was with them. Peter put all of them outside, and then he knelt down and prayed. He turned to the body and said, "Tabitha, get up." Then she opened her eyes, and seeing Peter, she sat up. He gave her his hand and helped her up. Then calling the saints and widows, he showed her to be alive. (Acts 9:36–41)

Since this is a book about women in faith-based community organizing, naturally there will be connections for these women between the work and their own faith. For many of them, myself included, the motivation to pursue an organizing career or avocation arose most directly out of our sense that this was the most authentic way to live out our faith values.

For me, pursuing some sort of church vocation was always in the cards. I grew up with the Lutheran church looming large, both literally and figuratively. In my most formative years, the church we attended was directly behind our back yard, across a small vacant field. My parents were active church leaders, close neighbors and friends attended, and my experience of church was almost entirely positive. Our pastors, though all male, were important role models who, on frequent occasions, noted and nurtured my gifts for ministry. That positive environment cultivated in me an enduring faith in an accessible God who was loving and just, in whose image I knew I was created.

A most formative experience was when our beloved youth pastor of many years started a twice-monthly contemporary worship service and drafted several of us youth, along with adults, as musicians and worship leaders. When

preparing to leave for a call to a new ministry, he invited me—then a junior
in high school—to replace him as the main leader of the group and coordinator of the service. The self-confidence that his invitation and that experience
provided was profound. No less profound of an impact came through the music that this pastor had introduced us to, mainly religious folk songs that had
social justice themes, many drawn from civil rights and protest movements.
Those themes inevitably worked their way into my psyche and the development of my values around justice and power.

I served as a parish pastor for sixteen years, but in hind-sight it seems
like it was inevitable that I would discover and fully pursue a career in
faith-based community organizing. I always kindled a justice point of view
in my preaching, teaching, and ministering. I moved along my pastoral
journey from youth pastor to neighborhood outreach pastor to social ministry pastor, until I discovered organizing. Eventually I left the parish to
work full-time in the faith-based community organizing field. For the past
fifteen years, it has served as the truest way for me to live out my faith in
the world.

Four other women described to me how faith led them to their affiliation
with organizing:

> I had wanted to find an expression of my own faith, having grown up as a
> pastor's kid. Organizing awakened in me a sense of faith as an active life,
> living out my values in the world. To be deeply connected with people,
> in their pain, in their joy, in their hope for change, walking actively with
> them.
>
> —eva schulte

> I really wanted to change the world. That comes out of my Unitarianism,
> but also my mother's Catholicism. I grew up with Catholic values: Don't
> talk about faith; do it. Help people, give rides, bring soup to the sick, help
> animals. It was deeply in me. Saving the world mattered to me.
>
> —Pamela Twiss

> I think what I experienced when I was an undergrad at St. Ben's fed
> something that I was searching for. The whole message of social justice,
> the concepts, the grounding of it in our faith; that it's so important to do
> justice. I heard what I was looking for then and I continued to look for that.
> That was the biggest driving force for me behind seeing organizing as a
> good mechanism to achieve what I wanted to do. I never went through a
> charity phase. I went right toward the root cause work.
>
> —Mary Gruber

I had wanted to be a rabbi since I was 13. When you want something for that long, it's easy to get a little lost in why and to what end and what it will look like. I grew up in a home that was really loving and compassionate and had all the good Reform Jewish values that we talked about: kindness to the vulnerable, etc. But I didn't know that there were groups of people who were trying to change stuff.

For whatever reason I was a very sensitive kid and it just broke my heart to see so many homeless people on the streets of New York. And I would cry, wondering when humanity got together and said, "Okay, some of us get to go home at night and others of us just don't get to go home." It looked to me like we had just decided that was reality!

I carried this on my shoulders for a long time. I was really pained about this, until I decided that I had to do something about it. I knew I couldn't just be sad.

—Stephanie Kolin

For seven of the women I interviewed, their faith and their affinity for organizing were shaped by certain explicit and foundational teachings or experiences from their upbringing in particular religious traditions:

I'd always been interested in social justice because of Catholic Social Teaching.

—Maureen Geddes

During college, I went on a Lutheran World Federation mission trip and learned about the kind of justice that the Lutheran church leads throughout this world.

—eva schulte

The stuff I learned working with Catholics showed me a higher purpose and the building of community. I also really loved their music and the sense of spirituality among them and their very clear commitment to social justice and equity. So I had the grace of the Lutherans and the clear expectations of the Catholics, their accountability. I needed both those things in my life.

—Meghan Sobocienski

When I became a Christian at fourteen, in a National Baptist Convention church, all I really knew about church was like Civil Rights and that Malcolm X was Muslim and he was a movement person. So I came into church thinking that I was sort of entering a Civil Rights documentary! My first pastor did a lot of community organizing and brought a lot of national level speakers in to talk and preach.

—Onleilove Alston

Religion played a role for me, even though my parents were not real devout Catholics. I always saw Jesus as revolutionary. I always thought about what Jesus would do. That was a moral compass for me. I was at a Catholic High School for part of my education. I did walks for hunger, that sort of thing. It became a part of my moral core. I sometimes drive other UUs crazy because I admit to being an unabashed Jesus lover!

—Susan Leslie

Growing up Lutheran, the Theology of the Cross has always been central for me. It's not just a construct. We know God most profoundly on the cross. God dwells most profoundly in the wounds of the world. Our wounds then are not something to be ashamed of, but the very space where God is present and active and at work. So to go to those spaces and places in our lives and stories and communities, we'll find God's liberative and creative power at work.

—Melissa Reed

When I was growing up in the Dominican Republic, my grandmother had a little booklet on Catholic Social Teaching—in Spanish. I thought every Catholic church must be following it, being out in the community, working to empower people and eliminate poverty, to build the kingdom on earth.

—Ana Garcia-Ashley

Searching for the Right Thing

Joshua . . . sent two men . . . as spies, saying, "Go, view the land, especially Jericho." So they went, and entered the house of a prostitute whose name was Rahab, and spent the night there. The king of Jericho was told, "Some Israelites have come here tonight to search out the land."

Then the king of Jericho sent orders to Rahab, "Bring out the men who have come to you, who entered your house, for they have come only to search out the whole land." But the woman took the two men and hid them. Then she said, "True, the men came to me, but I did not know where they came from. And when it was time to close the gate at dark, the men went out. Where the men went I do not know. Pursue them quickly, for you can overtake them . . . " So the men pursued them on the way to the Jordan as far as the fords.

As soon as the pursuers had gone out, the gate was shut . . . [Rahab] said to the men: "I know that the Lord has given you the land, and that dread of you has fallen on us, and that all the inhabitants of the land melt in fear before you . . . Now then, since I have dealt kindly with you, swear to me by the Lord that you in turn will deal kindly with my family. Give me a sign of good faith that you will spare my father and mother, my brothers and sisters, and all who belong to them, and deliver our lives from death."

The men said to her, "Our life for yours! If you do not tell this business of ours, then we will deal kindly and faithfully with you when the Lord gives us the land." (Joshua 2:1–14)

Not every woman who has found meaning through faith-based community organizing started out with that realm as her vehicle. In the quest for a meaningful life's pursuit, some turned to other outlets or career paths first. But in each case, they experienced a lack of fulfillment or longed for more effective means to meet their desired goals and express their deepest values. My own story from the section on faith above includes this sort of circuitous route, as do the accounts from my interviews of these five women:

In the last year of seminary, I was working for Interfaith Worker Justice and paired with AFL-CIO and SEIU. I would call on clergy and we'd focus on a living wage campaign in Richmond. I learned so much from the training I got in the labor environment. But I yearned for a model that was more values-driven, deeply rooted in faith communities, and how our faith values live in public life and form our methodology for systemic change.

Then I learned the language and the tools of organizing in a class at one of the consortium seminaries. I took it and I was just hooked; I had to be a community organizer! I finally had a label for what I wanted to be. I was hungry for that identity.

—eva schulte

When I graduated from college, I knew I wanted to be an agent of change. But I didn't know how to do it. Then one of my journalism professors told me about the documentary film program. So I applied. In my mind I thought that what I was going to do was to move to predominantly Black neighborhoods, predominantly poor neighborhoods, build some relationships, find out what people want their communities to look like, and help them create that by making a documentary film about their community. Then they could take that film to their local councils, mayors, whomever, to talk about the goodness of their community and about what the people living there want. So, instead of gentrifying them, for example, let's listen to what they want and let them be a part of what happens to their community. That was my vision.

In February of 2005 I'd gone through the program, I'd done my thesis film, I was applying to all these different places that made documentary films, trying to figure out what to do next. As president of a campus organization, I got an e-mail from a group that was recruiting on campus and was asking me to let my members know they were coming. It basically said, "Work with people in their local communities to get affordable housing, healthcare, better schools." And I was like, "WHAT? There's a career for just that? There's this thing you can do that's not behind the camera, but you can work with people in their communities so that they can improve it themselves?"

I went to the info session and here was the recruitment director at DART, Ben McConnell, talking about "the world as it is" vs. "the world as it should be." And how we can be a part of pulling those two together through organizing. He invited people back the next day if we wanted to be interviewed. I was on Cloud Nine!

I debated how I was going to talk with my parents. They'd had to borrow a lot of money to put me through grad school. And now I thought that I didn't want to make documentary films, for which I'd gone to school and borrowed all that money! I thought that I wanted to be a community organizer. I called them that night and I told them what I'd heard. And they were like, "That sounds just like you! That is awesome. We support your change in direction. Do it!" So I did.

—Leah Wiley

I met a guy at a party who started telling me about community organizing. And I had this sense that this was really an important conversation. The party fell away and I just felt called to pay attention. At the group home where I was working, I was helping a dozen individual kids. But the stuff that landed them at the group home, I wasn't doing anything about that. I wanted to do something about that.

—Pamela Twiss

I studied public policy in college and wanted to make a difference in the world. I got a job in the federal government, in the general accounting office in D.C. I was there two years, in the Department of Agriculture. I could see how the work I was doing could change policy and impact people's lives, but I had never met a farmer in my life! That didn't match where I wanted to be. It didn't feel relational enough.

Then I moved to California and got a Master's in City Planning at U.C. Berkeley. What I found at city planning school was almost the same thing on a smaller level; that cities often make policy decisions on behalf of people, with those people having no chance to be a part of that. It felt even more wrong, since there's more access to people on a local level.

So that's when I started to get curious about what community organizing was. Between my first two years of city planning school, I started looking for a chance to do some community organizing.

—Lydia Ferrante-Roseberry

I was 26 and living in Chicago, after finishing at the University of Chicago. I was doing theater for about four years. I was at an intersection of my own struggle to see myself as somebody who could be a respected, powerful person and my own history in my family and my upbringing and my politics. That stew of things was undigested. I was struggling to see myself as powerful. I wanted it, but I was scared of it and I couldn't see it.

Theater became the first manifestation of me trying to see myself in public. So I was doing theater and I was working at Morgan Stanley and Dean Witter as a temp; it was my day job.

Then I met a guy in my neighborhood who worked with the Alinsky-based Logan Square Neighborhood Association. I took a leap and I applied for an internship, an AmeriCorps position at a coalition of neighborhood-based groups.

But I quickly felt like neighborhood organizing was small and myopic and made up of fiefdoms. My feeling was that there had to be a bigger and deeper vision and story if we're going to save democracy.

—Doran Schrantz

Meeting Strangers Along the Way

Jesus left that place and went away to the district of Tyre and Sidon. Just then a Canaanite woman from that region came out and started shouting, "Have mercy on me, Lord, Son of David; my daughter is tormented by a demon." But he did not answer her at all. And his disciples came and urged him, saying, "Send her away, for she keeps shouting after us." He answered, "I was sent only to the lost sheep of the house of Israel."

But she came and knelt before him, saying, "Lord, help me." He answered, "It is not fair to take the children's food and throw it to the dogs." She said, "Yes, Lord, yet even the dogs eat the crumbs that fall from their masters' table." Then Jesus answered her, "Woman, great is your faith! Let it be done for you as you wish." And her daughter was healed instantly. (Matthew 15:21–32)

For many of the women I interviewed, it was an experience of encountering people who were very different from them, in terms of class or culture, that opened their eyes to the disparities and injustices around them. That exposure lit a fire within them to become agents of change, and to find the best vehicles by which to create that change. Here three of the women I interviewed describe how such encounters altered their worldview and life choices:

When I was living in Iowa, I did several summer jobs in the fields. One summer I worked with an organization that does job training for migrant workers. Waiting next to the fields for the workers to finish their work days, I saw their conditions, how they were living in terrible settings.

The second summer I translated for three women who had lost their babies or had babies who had severe respiratory issues or other physical malformation. That experience made me feel we had to do something, that these issues couldn't be accidental.

But there were no vehicles for working to change the systems that were so unjust and unhealthy for the workers. I didn't know that world, that there was a power dynamic that we could organize around. I wrote a paragraph for our organization's newsletter, but of course, it wasn't enough.

—eva schulte

I grew up in an upper middle-class town about an hour away from New York City. During high school, I had an experience or an epiphany of God, in going to the city for the very first time by myself in the early 1980s. I got off the bus and got on an escalator and started going down, and it was a sea of sleeping bags on the floor of the port authority, with Black faces peering out. I had an immediate knowing that my life was intimately connected to those lives. Try as the culture might to separate us into ethnic and class enclaves, that was not the case.

That experience never left me. It was an immediate understanding of one-ness or interconnection, an awakening to that. It wasn't pity; it was like, "We are one." I decided I would not live a life that would separate me from that.

—Lydia Ferrante-Roseberry

In 1986 we were at Gustavus Adolphus Lutheran in St. Paul. Through the Lutheran seminary we were offered this cross-cultural exchange experience. At first we hosted international students who were attending Luther Seminary; people from Guyana, India, Jordan. They spent six weeks studying at Luther and they spent the weekends at our congregations.

After that we were invited to go to India for a month. We spent that month going to churches, of course, but they also took us to the places where our benevolence money worked, the places where people are suffering from oppression. The poverty was in your face and you couldn't ignore it. I realized the poverty was here at home too, but one could choose to ignore it.

I came back from what was a transformative experience and I suffered in silent rage. My questions became: What do you do with these new feelings? What causes oppression? And why, in a country as old as India, is there so much of it? And how do you work for justice?

—Myrna Nelson

Prejudice in One's Own Life

Sarah saw the son of Hagar the Egyptian, whom she had borne to Abraham, playing with her son Isaac. So she said to Abraham, "Cast out this slave woman with her son; for the son of this slave woman shall not inherit along with my son Isaac . . . " So Abraham rose early in the morning, and took bread and a skin of water, and gave it to Hagar, putting it on her shoulder, along with the child, and sent her away. And she departed, and wandered about in the wilderness of Beer-sheba. (Genesis 21:9–10, 14)

Throughout this book I have made references to gender- or class-based bias as harsh realities for women in faith-based community organizing. For several of the women I interviewed, their experiences of being a woman, a person of color, a lesbian, or someone who grew up poor or working-class, have been powerful motivators on their paths toward becoming agents of their own destinies, and contributors to the empowerment of others. Onleilove Alston talks about how people tend to view these realities in their lives, and how organizing can bring a different perspective:

> A lot of times people blame themselves for their situation. And they don't see the way in which certain systems collapse opportunity for people, due to their race or their economic situation. Many faith traditions teach that when bad things happen, it's an individual's fault, and you're trying to save the individual soul.
>
> What I love about faith organizing is it recognizes that salvation is not individual, that the Messiah didn't just come for each individual person, but for the whole community.
>
> So for me, it's not about helping that one person get a job, or visiting one prisoner through the prison ministry. With faith organizing, you can scale up and say, "I'm tired of having to visit people in prison! I want to be able to visit people outside of prison! Why are there so many people in prison?"

Six others shared with me how their struggles with bias shaped them:

> One thing I did as a trainer early on is, I used to dress in layers. I never thought there was a rationale. But later I realized that it was my way of protecting myself. I had to wear my armor: scarves and jackets and dark clothes. I was terrified that the people were going to figure out who I really was, and they would laugh. I never overcame that. I was terrified every time. Because I wanted to do it so badly. But I had all these things working against me, my background, my lack of education, my poverty. I had to create another personality. Because if I sent me, I'd cry! I'd get too scared. I had to create another way of being and dressing; a mask. Nobody could penetrate that. I had to wear that because I was afraid.

—Mary Gonzales

In my own family system there was a lot of sexism. I felt disempowered as a woman in my family. My parents are Italian immigrants and so my dad is like the typical Italian patriarch, everything run around him. There was

sexism in how my brothers were treated and how I was treated. I think that
was an internalized oppression. I never translated it into work on women's
issues, which I think for me is because it was too intimate to touch the
oppression there. But I did translate it into issues of class; my organizing
work was around class a lot.

—Lydia Ferrante-Roseberry

I had wanted to be a pastor. I went to Gettysburg Seminary, but was outed
in my first semester. In the '70s that meant that it was better for me to
leave. But my learnings from that experience contributed every day to my
work in the church. Without that, it looks very different.

—Emily Eastwood

I grew up Catholic working-class in South Bend, Indiana. My father
worked three jobs to put food on the table. When the owner there was
thinking of moving the plant, I got my wake-up call to what power was.
My father was nearly laid off and then he got sick and I realized that, wow,
we did not have agency! Because of the type of work and the economics
of it. I was about nine years old.

Three years later, I had the experience of being victimized. That feeling
of powerlessness on top of feeling the powerlessness of my father made
me turn into a victim, in every imaginable way.

Well, in my Catholic high school there was a class I took on the prophets. I felt like I was hearing for the first time the message about this Jewish
God caring about the widow and the orphan. I felt like *I* was the widow
and the orphan!

Those feelings of powerlessness really launched me toward organizing.
It was totally out of self-interest, not wanting to feel powerless anymore,
moving out of my victimhood mentality.

—Jeannie Appleman

My father and grandfather were pastors. I wanted to be a pastor too. But
I understood early on that I was different from them. I knew that my
vocation as a wife and mother would change almost everything as far as
relating to church, how my life would have requirements to it that were
different from them, just because I was female. I was wakening to being a
woman in a male-dominated and male-defined institution.

I also worked in banking in New York for about four and a half years
and I understood sexism in the business environment. That gave me more
of an understanding of being on the margins of an institution, both the
struggle of that and the possibility of that.

I learned about sexism also when I was an athlete in high school and
college and really learned to protest when those of us who played softball
had to walk a half a mile to our field and the boys' field was right outside.

I think it just gave me a sense of how not being at the center of things and how they were planned and organized, that got my attention and I had a kinship with others on the edge or marginalized. I began to understand who has power and who doesn't have power.

—Karen Brau

As I came of age, I started to dread coming into church spaces, because everything was very traditionally gendered. I was starting to understand my attraction to women and I knew that wasn't going to be acceptable in those spaces. College also exposed me to some of the cultural perspectives of the church, and how sexist and heterosexist the institution of the church, and even of marriage, is.

Later on though, I got to know a Lutheran pastor, Katrina Foster, who is a lesbian. And this started to change my perspective about faith. Candace and I were starting to think about getting married and I was interested in that being a church wedding. I asked Katrina to counsel us and officiate at our service. She agreed and told us we were her first-ever same-sex couple to work with in that way. That helped shape my formation.

—Louisa Fletcher-Pacheco

Politics, Movements, and World Events

When the queen of Sheba heard of the fame of Solomon, (fame due to the name of the Lord), she came to test him with hard questions. She came to Jerusalem with a very great retinue, with camels bearing spices, and very much gold, and precious stones; and when she came to Solomon, she told him all that was on her mind. Solomon answered all her questions; there was nothing hidden from the king that he could not explain to her . . .

So she said to the king, "The report was true that I heard in my own land of your accomplishments and of your wisdom, but I did not believe the reports until I came and my own eyes had seen it. Not even half had been told me; your wisdom and prosperity far surpass the report that I had heard . . . "

Then she gave the king one hundred twenty talents of gold, a great quantity of spices, and precious stones; never again did spice come in such quantity as that which the queen of Sheba gave to King Solomon. (1 Kings 10:1–3, 6–7, 10)

Beyond personal experiences of prejudice, many women who are active in faith-based organizing came to it in part because of their exposure to particular political arena realities or as a result of catastrophic events on the world stage. Here are five examples from my interviews:

In high school I was chosen to go to Girls' State, where you go to the university for a week or ten days, and you form cities and counties and government, where people get elected. That was a good learning experience.

Then when I was a junior, my friend and I took a senior class called Problems of Democracy. I found that really interesting, too. It was kind of analyzing democracy. At one point you had to study the constitution and take a test. I got the best score! The seniors were miffed that a junior got the best score! But my interest in government was always there.

—Myrna Nelson

I had always thought that, once the rules [about gay ordination] changed, I'd leave corporate work and go back to seminary and become a pastor.

But watching the towers fall on 9/11, my response was immediate and defensive, in the moment, which really surprised me. There was no ethical dilemma for me that you have to sacrifice the few for the many. I didn't sleep for days. The people in the fourth plane were the ones who took action and made sure it didn't go where it was supposed to go. That would have been me. I would not have been sitting cowering in my chair. I would have been organizing.

9/11 showed me that I could run out of time. Our sense of security in this country was an illusion. There was no defense system that would protect us. Our life was never going to be the same.

—Emily Eastwood

I was reading Hannah Arendt, who was a Jewish philosopher. She was basically writing about public life and totalitarianism as a woman who escaped Nazi Germany. A lot of American-based community organizing comes out of her framework. I didn't know that, but I was reading her book "On Revolution" and she was writing about the American, French, and Russian revolutions.

And I loved this book so much, it would make me weep! It was her descriptions of what it meant to feel fully human and what creates that capacity. What makes people human? Her argument is that it's politics, with a small "p." It's the entering of a public sphere where you and others meet each other to create the world, the political body.

I was reading that and I also saw, on Labor Day in Chicago, the showing of "Democracy's Promise," about Saul Alinsky. It also just made me weep. I was looking for something, and those two things lined up, and I saw that there was a way to put this into practice. There was something about organizing and the way that it described how people could relate to each other; not top-down, not "I'm an expert" or a technocrat or a consumer. It felt right, so I started exploring organizing.

—Doran Schrantz

When I went to college, I got involved in the Black Caucus, because that was something you did socially as a Black student. There was a fraternity and sorority fair and some people I knew were promoting a historically Black fraternity at the fair. Their picture from the fair was put over a story in the student newspaper about a robbery, instead of the story about the fraternity fair. It made it look like these two young Black men robbed someone!

So the president of the Black Caucus at the time did an editorial about racial bias. The newspaper apologized; everyone thought it was a learning moment, right? But then I was sitting in one of our meetings and the president opened up a letter and it was hate mail addressed to her; then Black football players started getting hate mail; then their parents started getting hate mail.

So we started protesting and organizing and becoming activists. We ended up taking over the student union building and having something called The Village, which got into the national news. Students of all backgrounds occupied the building because, as a state school, they were obligated to serve the Black students of the Commonwealth of Pennsylvania, and they weren't doing that.

So we created a campaign holding Penn State accountable based on their own constitution. We threatened to go to the capitol, knowing the university got a lot of money from the state. There was negotiation with the school administration. We got a lot of our demands met; a lot more diversity at Penn State happened. All of that was my first example of the power of organizing. We were really changed by that experience.

—Onleilove Alston

While in college, my heart was in the protest movements of united Mexican-American students. It was a very politicizing time for me. I was a women's studies and ethnic studies major and I was studying movements and then practicing them in my school.

The professors in my women's studies and ethnic studies departments came to our student organization asking for help because they weren't getting tenure. They wanted the students to know there was no track for us, as people of color, to go into academia ourselves. They asked for our help and that's when I started getting politicized. We wanted to make sure they had equal rights and an equal shot at tenure. So we got in the streets.

We organized a protest. I remember creating this amazing poster that made the front page of the student newspaper. We knew we needed a target—a decision maker. We knew that the president at the time was the person who could make this change. So we had one of the largest protests in Boulder in a long time, since the 70s.

Relatively quickly the president decided to create a track for those professors to get tenure. I saw that organizing was the thing that got things to move and change. It was really defining for me.

—Louisa Fletcher-Pacheco

Politicizing One's Pain

> Now there was a woman who had been suffering from hemorrhages for twelve years; and though she had spent all she had on physicians, no one could cure her. She came up behind Jesus and touched the fringe of his clothes, and immediately her hemorrhage stopped. Then Jesus asked, "Who touched me?" When all denied it, Peter said, "Master, the crowds surround you and press in on you." But Jesus said, "Someone touched me; for I noticed that power had gone out from me." When the woman saw that she could not remain hidden, she came trembling; and falling down before him, she declared in the presence of all the people why she had touched him, and how she had been immediately healed. He said to her, "Daughter, your faith has made you well; go in peace." (Luke 8:43–48)

In organizing, there's a concept we refer to as politicizing your pain or politicizing your anger or oppression. It may start coming into focus during a session on self-interest early in the week of community organizing training. It involves getting in touch with your own life story and those events and circumstances that have led you to this particular point and place in time. While considering your array of self-interests that lead you to care about the kinds of issues we address in faith-based community organizing, trainers encourage you to explore how your own life has been touched, or sometimes even dictated, by misfortune or injustice.

Sometime during the week of training, participants may take part in an exercise that brings them even deeper into their own story, where they are encouraged to identify the deepest pain or oppression—perhaps even their most formidable oppressor—that has had the greatest impact on their self-identity and value system. As people begin to name these factors, trainers and fellow trainees help one another shift the narrative away from self-pity and helplessness. Together we begin to understand that most of our pain and oppression is not a result of our own poor choices, but is instead tied to larger systems and cultural narratives. And, we begin to see that we are not as alone as we thought we were in our struggles, as others' stories ring familiar and true, fostering a sense of community and collective power.

The idea of *politicizing* one's pain, anger, or oppression is introduced as how one can begin to harness these dynamics into collective public action. In the current era, one pithy way this concept is expressed is, "Don't mourn; organize!"

Here five women describe how their own experiences with pain, personal crisis, oppression, or other harsh life realities served as fuel for the flame of justice burning within them:

> I was arrested and incarcerated and facing ten years in prison for arson of an inhabited structure. I don't remember the details, because I had

never stopped drinking. When I try to think back, now that I'm sober, a lot of my life is darkness and a blur; nothing. So, I was facing ten years, but I was able to cut a deal with the district attorney. I had to spend time in a county detention facility for one year and be registered as an arsonist.

My first day incarcerated, a roommate gave me a Bible. She told me to start from the beginning. A week later I was saved in Bible study and I read it from cover to cover. The Bible itself introduced me to a different God than I had known before. That night after she gave me the Bible, I laid in bed and I thought, well I'm just going to try this. I asked, "Lord, please take the taste and need and want of alcohol away from me and help me." Then I laid there and cried and started reading. It made so much sense! God really spoke to me! After that, I didn't have to detox. I had a hangover and that was it. I read the Bible every day and finished in a month and a half. I read every page, every word.

The God that I was learning about and who was showing up for me was not this punishing judgmental God. It was a God that told me that "When I return everything to you, nobody will be able to take it away." I really heard that, just knowing that God wouldn't put me through all of this for nothing. It made me recognize that I was still alive because God has always been in my life, waiting for me. I now had somebody to turn everything over to.

—Tamisha Walker

At weeklong training, Mary Gonzales did a session on agitation. The interactions seemed really crazy to me! Then when a bunch of people showed up late to a training session and John Norton screamed at them; that's when I decided I was going to leave.

But that day I turned into a different person. I called my mom and she asked me if I was scared. I said, "Yes, I guess so." She said "Don't be like me. When I was young, I didn't do anything!" I just remember thinking that I was going to throw up. And I did! But the minute I did, I felt different; I was seeing things differently.

I remember the trainers saying a lot of things about power. And I thought, "This isn't for me." But when my mom created that space for me, in our conversation, I thought, "Why not? Why do I have to wait for someone else to do this job?"

I remember thinking then that this did have to do with me being a parent. I realized that this connected to what I wanted as a parent, this kind of work. It felt like I could change the world and a culture of people who see me a certain way. It was scary and I wasn't sure I was up for the lifestyle. But once I felt this calling, I knew I could not go back.

—Mary Lim-Lampe

I was in my fourth year of school and ordination was speeding towards me and I didn't have a shape to my rabbinate. I didn't have a vision or focus of what it would look like in a way that would be meaningful for me and ways that I could best contribute to the world, to the Reform movement, to Jews, to non-Jews.

That was happening at the same time that I was starting to feel really hopeless in my work in the soup kitchen. It was a wonderful place, but it started to become really clear that the same people had been coming like sixteen and seventeen years!

One evening a man came to our clothing line and I went to check on our guests and he asked me if I had a winter coat for him. I noticed that he was already wearing one, so I asked him if that one just wasn't working for him. It was January and it was cold and wind was just ripping through clothing. He said that he had been arrested earlier that week for public urination. People didn't want him in their establishment to use the restroom because he looked a bit shabby and disheveled. So what is he supposed to do? So he gets arrested, they take him to the jail, and the policy was to cut his shoelaces and to take the strings out of his jacket. Now if you can't cinch your jacket in this weather, the wind will just cut right up it and it's really quite useless. But they brought him in and then sent him back out worse off than they brought him in!

The reason they cut the strings on the jacket and the shoelaces is in case he's a suicide risk. I asked him if he was thinking about killing himself. And he said, "Lady, I just had to pee!" So we found him a jacket that would work, and I went to our storage room and just fell apart. It was so sad and so unfair!

My head chef came in and I told him what had happened. I said, "That's it! I'm going to call the jail and tell them the policy is bad!" And he hugged me as any good friend would and told me to let him know if I got past the front desk. And that was a generous thought.

I didn't even know what jail to call or what I would say when they picked up the phone. I had no idea what any of this meant. And I felt powerless for the first time in my life. I had been powerless my entire life, but I understood it now. I really felt it deep.

—Stephanie Kolin

The most powerful "aha" for me was around my eating disorder that I'd had when I was in college, which I'd never really touched or confronted. I had been very depressed after a breakup and very susceptible to the high-pressure culture of Boston academia and lots of money, wealth, and beauty. As a young woman those messages really got to me. I think what happened was that I stopped eating because I was depressed, but then I got positive feedback from everyone around me about losing weight. So that became something I could control.

I'd gotten a lot healthier since then, but I don't think I'd ever really dealt with those messages that had driven me. I carried a lot of shame around that.

But then during my pastoral internship, I was in this congregation full of people who knew their stories and knew how to share them and how to invite your story. All these people who were being vulnerable and connecting the dots of their own stories to the systemic and public and collective story. It made me really examine my own story and where the pressures were. The liberative nature of that—that this just wasn't my issue or my problem—that was significant.

—Melissa Reed

Organizing out of deep-rooted pain and sorrow has become really important to me after the stillbirth of my son Lincoln. Prophetic justice doesn't mean much without the pastoral pain of where our people are. Sharing our own stories allows us to continue.

Too often, though, we put our stories in our back pockets and we don't necessarily authentically relate with those we're working with. So for example, life expectancy is the focus in the hot-spot neighborhoods where we are organizing. And I don't think I would have fully understood life expectancy if not for my loss. It allowed me to recognize the race disparities and also how close we all are to loss.

—eva schulte

POWER TO PERSIST

In every day and age, ordinary people, like the women featured in this book, must find the power, along with steadfast persistence, to address the pressing challenges they face in their lives and in their communities and cultures. Our time is no different, though for those of us living in it, it certainly seems more intensely daunting than ever! Understanding how others have risen to the challenges can help us muster the courage, companions, and resources to face our own.

The twenty-one women, plus myself, that I have introduced to you in this book come from diverse backgrounds, representing a range of ages, adhering to a variety of faith expressions, and having had vastly different life experiences. But each found her way to, or was found along the way by, faith-based community organizing. That encounter, and each woman's embrace of the tools and methodologies, led her to become personally more powerful as well as publicly more influential. Each in her own way recognized the movement of the Divine, compelling her to embrace her individual as well as collective power. What each woman discovered about herself along the way clarified what she wanted to do and who she wanted to be in the world.

WHAT DO YOU BRING?

In chapters 1 and 4 I told about the training program, called Ntosake, that the Gamaliel organization provides for women. I mentioned that the word Ntosake means "she who walks with lions and carries her own things." The meaning of that word is profound when you consider the lion-like courage women have to muster to make their way in a world that is still so much the domain of men. And it means so much to comprehend that we have our own things—our own assets, faults, insights, fears, talents, wounds, and power—to bring to the task of authentic living, courageous action, and beloved community.

Marianne Williamson wrote, in her book *A Return to Love*, a paragraph that has become one of my own sacred texts. It speaks to the deeply personal desire and decision to embrace our God-given power and uniqueness in ways that reverberate well beyond our individual selves:

> Our deepest fear is not that we are inadequate. Our deepest fear is that we are powerful beyond measure. It is our light, not our darkness that most frightens us. We ask ourselves, "Who am I to be brilliant, gorgeous, talented, fabulous?" Actually, who are you not to be? You are a child of God. Your playing small does not serve the world. There is nothing enlightened about shrinking so that other people won't feel insecure around you. We are all meant to shine, as children do. We were born to make manifest the glory of God that is within us. It's not just in some of us; it's in everyone. And as we let our own light shine, we unconsciously give other people permission to do the same. As we are liberated from our own fear, our presence automatically liberates others.[1]

The clarity gained by each of the women you've met in this book came in part through the courageous questions other people asked, and that she asked of herself, about her life, her values, her vision, and her motivations. Each of us can gain greater clarity and courage to become more fully who we were created to be, and to do more intentionally what we are called to do. We can discover and celebrate what all we bring to this fraught and noble enterprise of life. But it takes intention and investment and a willingness to go deep, with ourselves and with others we trust and invite to go with us.

When I provide introductory training about discovering one's own self-interests—those things that have shaped us into who we are and that motivate us still—I ask people to reflect and write in response to a broad set of probing questions. I leave my readers to ponder some of these questions as a simple starting point in considering how to respond to these chapters:

- What, from your family, your education, your work, or volunteerism, has shaped you?
- What ambitions, dreams, and hopes have you had, and how have you tried to achieve them?
- What disappointments or barriers have you had to face, and how and with whom have you dealt with them?
- When have you felt most powerful and when have you felt least powerful, and why?
- What roles have religion, politics, race, class, gender, or sexual orientation played for you?
- What kind of impact do you want to have on your community, and why? How's it going?
- What do you do in your "down time," and with whom and why do you choose those things?
- What do you value, and why, so much so that you would publicly defend it? Have you done so?
- What are you most fearful about, that perhaps keeps you from acting more boldly?
- What does it take, or what will it take, to get you out of your fearfulness and into action?
- What do you bring (and will you bring it?) into the divine and noble call to do justice?

Each of us is but one person. But each of us is surrounded by others, whether already known to us or not, who yearn to be agents of change for the sake of that divine and noble call. The women encountered through this book have discovered their power, and their companions, for that work. May my readers as well find the courage and the resolve to take bold action in answer to that call.

NOTE

1. Marianne Williamson, *A Return to Love* (New York: Harper Collins, 1992), 190–91.

Biographical Profiles of the Women Interviewed for This Book

Onleilove Chika Alston is the founder of *Prophetic Whirlwind: Uncovering the Black Biblical Destiny*, dedicated to educating people of faith on the Black Presence in the Bible. She is the former Executive Director of Faith in New York, a Faith in Action (formerly PICO) affiliate. Alston holds a Bachelor's degree in Human Development and African-American studies from Penn State University, a Master of Divinity degree from Union Theological Seminary, and a Master of Social Work degree from Columbia University School of Social Work. She is a visiting professor at the Liberia Baptist Theological Seminary and a contributing writer for *Sojourners* magazine, The Black Commentator, Huffington Post, and National Public Radio's Onbeing blog.

Jeannie Appleman is a senior organizer and trainer at Jewish Organizing Institute and Network (JOIN) for Justice, which strengthens the community organizing practice of Jewish organizers, leaders, and organizations so that the Jewish community can effectively play a role in the social justice struggles of our country. Appleman trains seminary students in organizing, congregational development, and leadership. She also trains and develops synagogue leaders from all four of the Jewish movements in America. Previously she served as the lead organizer for the Industrial Areas Foundation's (IAF) affiliates in Long Island and Queens, and trained synagogue leaders in IAF's Westchester New York affiliate.

Karen Brau is the Senior Pastor of Luther Place Memorial Lutheran Church in Washington, D.C. Prior to coming to Luther Place in 2008, she served for eighteen years as a pastor in the inner city of Baltimore, where she was instrumental in forming Amazing Grace Lutheran Church and the Amazing Port Street Project. She was introduced to faith-based community organizing while earning her Master of Divinity degree from Louisville Presbyterian Theological Seminary. She became a practitioner in the field through a Gamaliel affiliate while serving in Baltimore. Brau is active in Washington Interfaith Network (WIN), an IAF affiliate organization.

Emily Eastwood served as Executive Director of Lutherans Concerned/ North America (now ReconcilingWorks) from 2004 to 2014. In that capacity she led strategic efforts to enable policy changes within the Evangelical Lutheran Church in America (ELCA) allowing for the ordination of lesbian, gay, bisexual, and transgender candidates in committed same-gender relationships and allowing for the marriage of same-gender couples. Policy changes were made by the ELCA in 2009. Eastwood was the first in the Lutheran community to adapt the principles of faith-based community organizing to the issue of LGBT inclusion in church. She retired in 2014.

Lydia Ferrante-Roseberry is the Senior Minister at Boulder Valley Unitarian Universalist Fellowship in Lafayette, Colorado. Previously she served as a community organizer for a PICO (now Faith in Action) affiliate in San Francisco, as a minister for social justice at Eden United Church of Christ in Hayward, California, and as a consulting minister at Chico Unitarian Universalist Fellowship in Chico, California. She holds a Bachelor of Science degree in Public Policy from Cornell University in New York, a Master's degree in City Planning from the University of California at Berkeley, and a Master of Divinity degree from Starr King School for the Ministry in Berkeley.

Louisa Fletcher-Pacheco is the Western New York Regional political organizer for New York State United Teachers, a union of over 600,000 people who work in, or are retired from, New York's schools, colleges, and healthcare facilities. She previously served as Executive Director of the Gamaliel national network's Western New York organization. She is a career organizer, having spent nearly twenty years transforming people's lives and the policies that impact them. She believes in true leadership development that has resulted while working on people's campaigns from Tenant Petition Inspections to dropping the Rockefeller Drug Laws in Albany to flipping the school board in Buffalo.

Ana Garcia-Ashley is the Executive Director of Gamaliel, the first woman and person of color to head a national organizing network. An immigrant from the Dominican Republic, she attended Catholic and public schools in the South Bronx, then moved to New Mexico to study at Highlands University. She graduated from the University of Colorado in Denver and then organized for Metropolitan Organization for People of Denver, a PICO affiliate (now Faith in Action). She attended the Iliff School of Theology to develop a foundation for organizing congregations. In the early 1990s she became Lead Organizer of Milwaukee Inner-City Congregations Allied for Hope (MICAH), a Gamaliel affiliate. During her tenure there, she was the founding organizer for WISDOM, the Gamaliel-affiliated Wisconsin statewide organization.

Maureen Geddes is a retired Catholic lay woman who spent much of her life as a professional community organizer, first with the Catholic Archdiocese of St. Paul and Minneapolis, then with ISAIAH of Minnesota. She was drawn to organizing in a faith-based coalition because of the necessity of moving faith into action. The joy of seeing leaders grow and live out their call is what kept her organizing for twenty years. Geddes is a graduate of St. Catherine University in Minnesota.

Mary Gonzales is a retired community organizer and trainer who co-founded and worked for the Gamaliel national network for twenty-eight years. During her tenure with Gamaliel, she created affiliate organizations; recruited, mentored, and trained organizers; provided training programs and support for religious leaders and laity; assisted in raising budgets; and developed breakthrough issue campaigns. She also founded Ntosake, a leadership training program specifically designed by and for women in the Gamaliel network. She continues to serve as a trainer, consultant, and mentor to Gamaliel organizers and organizations around the country.

Mary Gruber is a Catholic lay woman who works as a Clinical Nurse Specialist for HealthEast Care System in St. Paul, Minnesota. From 2004 to 2008 Gruber served as president of the board of ISAIAH of Minnesota, a Faith in Action (formerly PICO) affiliate. Gruber served as the co-chair of Gamaliel's National Leadership Assembly and founder and chair of Gamaliel's board of presidents. She was instrumental in the shaping of Ntosake, Gamaliel's premier training program for women. Gruber holds a Master's degree in nursing from Winona State University.

Stephanie Kolin is a rabbi at Central Synagogue in Manhattan, New York. From 2010 to 2015 she served as co-director of Just Congregations, the community organizing strategy of the Reform Movement, striving to enable faith communities to act powerfully together to create the change they want to see in the world. During this time she was lead organizer and founder of Reform California, the first-ever campaign of California Reform congregations to act together on issues of common concern. Her first congregation was Temple Israel in Boston. She co-founded the community organizing course at Hebrew Union College–Jewish Institute of Religion and has served as an adjunct professor at HUC.

Susan Leslie is the Congregational Advocacy and Witness Director for the Unitarian Universalist Association (UUA). She represents the UUA on the national board of Interfaith Worker Justice and on the Steering Committee of the Interfaith Organizing Initiative (IOI). Prior to her service at the UUA, Susan worked in publishing at Harvard University Press and Banner Press. She has a long history in community organizing. She held staff positions with Volunteers in Service to America (VISTA), the New Hampshire People's Alliance, the New England Municipal Center, and the Refuse and Resist Campaign. She holds a Bachelor of Arts degree in political science from the University of New Hampshire.

Mary Lim-Lampe is the Executive Director of Genesis, an affiliate of the Gamaliel national network in Oakland, California. Her passion is working with leaders to uncover their talents that have been squashed by oppression, discrimination, and racism. Previously she was a community organizer and Executive Director for MORE² (Metro Organization for Racial and Economic Equity), the Gamaliel affiliate in Kansas City, Missouri. She is a graduate of the University of Missouri-St. Louis and has a juris doctorate from St. Louis University-School of Law.

Myrna Nelson is a retired Lutheran lay woman who, in 1991, helped found what is now the ISAIAH organization of Minnesota, a Faith in Action (formerly PICO) affiliate. During her time with ISAIAH, she has served on its board of directors, and chaired numerous local and state-wide issue campaigns, as well as two on the federal level, relating to the civil rights of immigrants and United States funding for AIDS treatment in South Africa. She has served as a trainer for the Gamaliel network's Ntosake initiative, both in the United States and South Africa. She is a member of Lutheran Church of the Redeemer in St. Paul, Minnesota, an active ISAIAH member congregation.

Melissa Reed is the pastor at Salt and Light Lutheran Church and co-organizer of the Leaven Community in Portland, Oregon. She first learned about community organizing while earning her Master of Divinity degree at Pacific Lutheran Theological Seminary in Berkeley, California. She considers the principles and tools of organizing as foundational in her ministry. Salt and Light is a member of MACG, Metropolitan Alliance for the Common

Good, Portland's IAF affiliate, and IMIJ, Interfaith Movement for Immigrant Justice. Leaven Community is building a coalition of faith institutions seeking to collectively build affordable housing on the land of faith communities and pressuring city government around housing justice.

Doran Schrantz is the Executive Director of ISAIAH of Minnesota, a state-wide affiliate of the Faith in Action (formerly PICO) national network. She was instrumental in launching Healthy Heartlands, a five-state collaborative working at the intersection of the social determinants of health and democracy-building, staging strategic interventions which reduce health inequities. She is a graduate of the University of Chicago and an alumni of the Rockwood year-long Leadership from the Inside Out program. In 2012 she received the Young Leader Award from the Robert Wood Johnson Foundation, which recognized ten leaders under forty who are innovating around health and health care.

eva kathleen schulte is a Deacon in the Evangelical Lutheran Church in America (ELCA). She serves as vice president for economic opportunity at Travois, a mission-driven business headquartered in Kansas City. She supports impact investments through foundations and denominations to advance funds for housing and economic development within American Indian, Alaska Native, and Native Hawaiian communities. A long-time community organizer, eva was a state director and national consulting director with PICO (now Faith in Action). She served twelve years as President and CEO of Communities Creating Opportunity in Kansas City. She holds a Master of Arts degree from the Graduate Theological Union in Berkeley, California.

Meghan Sobocienski is a Deacon in the Evangelical Lutheran Church in America (ELCA). She is co-founder and Executive Director of Grace in Action Collectives, a partner of Grace in Action Church. Grace in Action Collectives is a network of four youth-run businesses that have created more than twenty-five worker-owners in Southwest Detroit. From 2010–2016, Meghan was a staff coordinator for the ELCA's Organizing for Mission Cohort. Previously she was an organizer with PICO (now Faith in Action), three years in California and two in Detroit. She holds a Master of Divinity degree from Pacific Lutheran Theological Seminary in Berkeley, California.

Pamela Twiss is the Director of Training at People's Action, a national network of grassroots organizations fighting for racial, social, and economic justice. She has worked in grassroots organizing and training for thirty-two years, on the staffs of low-income organizations, progressive political groups, labor unions, and faith-based organizations, including twelve years with ISAIAH of Minnesota, where she served as founding co-director. She earned her Bachelor of Arts degree from St. Anselm College in New Hampshire and studied for a Master's degree at the School for International Training in Vermont.

Tamisha Walker is Executive Director of Safe Return, a campaign to secure the freedom and liberation of formerly incarcerated individuals. Safe Return is a project of Contracosta Interfaith, a Faith in Action (formerly PICO) affiliate. Walker has been a community organizer and known advocate on issues related to mass incarceration and racial disparity in the criminal justice system since her release from incarceration in 2009. She holds a degree in psychology from Contra Costa Community College. Her educational experience also includes professional training in research and advocacy for the formerly incarcerated and their families, violence prevention strategies, and conflict mediation to reduce urban gun violence.

Leah Woodward Wiley is the Training and Development Director for DART (Direct Action and Research Training Center), a position she has held since 2011. Previously she was Senior Organizer for DART's Florida affiliate FAST (Faith in Action for Strength Together, in the St. Petersburg/Clearwater, Florida area), where she assisted and led several successful issue campaigns. She has a BA from Florida A & M University and a Master's of Mass Communication from the University of Florida. She intended to become a documentary film-maker, until, just after getting her Master's degree, she was introduced to DART. She discovered the power of organizing and recognized the limitations of consciousness-raising without action. Since then, she has not looked back!

Glossary of Terms
and Organizations

Agitation An accountability technique employed by trainers, organizers, and leaders, meant to provoke a response out of a subject by pointing out the disconnect between one's stated values or intentions and one's actual behavior. An effective agitation leads to a commitment from the person agitated to better align their behavior with their values and intentions.

Core Team (Also known as Justice Ministry or Local Organizing Committee) That select group of leaders that coordinates the congregation's relationship with its local community organizing affiliate. Core team members are encouraged to attend community organizing training, build strategic relationships in their own and other affiliate congregations, identify issues that directly affect them and their neighbors, and join in the actions of the affiliate to bring about the desired change, for the sake of greater equity and justice.

DART (Direct Action and Research Training Center) A national faith-based community organizing network, founded in 1982, with its headquarters in Miami Shores, Florida. DART has twenty-one affiliate organizations in eight U.S. states. DART affiliates "bring people together across racial, religious and socioeconomic lines to pursue justice in their communities, responding to God's call to do justice and redeem fallen systems" (from the DART website, www.thedartcenter.org).

External Listening Process See "Outreach."

Faith in Action (Formerly PICO) A national faith-based community organizing network, founded in 1972 as the Pacific Institute for Community Organizing, later People Improving Communities through Organizing, with

147

its headquarters in Oakland, California. Faith in Action has thirty-nine affiliate organizations (called federations) in twenty-one U.S. states and three other countries. Through its federated organizations, Faith in Action "engages large numbers of people through trusted community institutions to speak prophetically about the moral dimensions of political choices, bringing people together across race, class, religion, urban/suburban/rural, and region to make progress on racial and economic justice" (from the Faith in Action website, www.faithinaction.org).

Gamaliel   A national faith-based community organizing network, founded in 1986, with its headquarters in Chicago, Illinois. Gamaliel has forty-four affiliate organizations in seventeen U.S. states. Its mission is to "empower ordinary people to effectively participate in the political, environmental, social, and economic decisions affecting their lives. Gamaliel's diverse members apply their faith and values to the pursuit of equal opportunity for all, shared abundance, and stronger, more prosperous communities" (from the Gamaliel website, www.gamaliel.org).

House Meeting   A relatively small gathering of people, often members of one religious congregation, sometimes including non-member neighbors. A house meeting is designed to build and deepen relationships and uncover the interests and concerns of participants regarding their congregation, neighborhood, or broader community. When common interests and concerns surface, participants explore possible actions they might take collectively to create solutions.

IAF (Industrial Areas Foundation)   A national community organizing network, founded in 1940, with its headquarters in Chicago, Illinois. IAF has sixty affiliate organizations in twenty-two U.S. states, the District of Columbia, and four other countries. IAF affiliates "partner with religious congregations and civic organizations at the local level to build broad-based organizing projects which create new capacity in a community for leadership development, citizen-led action, and relationships across the lines that often divide our communities" (from the IAF website, www.industrialareasfoundation.org).

Inreach   (Also known as a Listening Campaign or Listening Season)
A coordinated effort to build relationships and listen deeply within one's congregation to as many ministry participants as possible. A team of listeners is trained in and commissioned to do one-to-ones with several others, during a 4–6 week time frame. At the end of the listening process, the listeners gather to identify the common themes they heard in their conversations. Those themes can lead a congregation into new ministry directions or into collective action around a shared concern in the congregation or broader community.

Intersectionality The concept that overlapping dynamics of gender, race, sexual identity, immigration status, and/or class that exist for many people in society contribute to greater and more complex levels of injustice or discrimination against such people.

Issue Campaign A strategic process by which a group of people identifies an issue of mutual concern and then works together to change public policy or corporate practice to create a more equitable system, one that provides greater access or resources to more people in any given community, region, state, or country.

Justice Ministry See "Core Team."

Leadership Training Each national organizing network conducts annual or more frequent training events that introduce leaders to the tools and principles of faith-based community organizing. These range from a week to ten days in duration, depending on the network. Among the topics covered are power, self-interest, one-to-ones, team building, effective meetings, power analysis, issues and actions, strategic campaigns, agitation, and money. Participants are challenged not only to acquire the basic tools, but also to grapple with what gets in their way of being powerful and effective leaders.

Listening Campaign or Listening Season See "Inreach."

Local Organizing Committee See "Core Team."

Mass Incarceration A term that describes the fact that the United States currently imprisons more of its population than any other country in the world, at any time in history. The number of people incarcerated has rapidly accelerated in the past forty-five years, from 200,000 in 1972 to approximately 2.3 million today. The term also is referenced with regard to the disproportionate number of people of color, Blacks in particular, who are incarcerated at a much higher per capita rate than those from the White population. Mass incarceration continues, despite the fact that the overall crime rate in the United States has declined steadily to about half of what it was in 1991. (Information gleaned from the Equal Justice Initiative website, www.eji.org.)

One-to-One Relational Meeting A conversation, about forty-five minutes in length, in which a trained listener invites another person to share deeply about their values, their vision, their life, and their motivations. The aim of the listener is to initiate or deepen a relationship with the other person and to uncover those things that matter most to that person. The listener does this by asking respectful but probing questions and eliciting stories that illustrate the person's experiences and the values and vision they hold.

Outreach   A coordinated external listening process to build relationships in the neighborhood where a congregation is situated. An organizing outreach is different from a traditional outreach, where the intent is to invite neighbors to come to services or religious activities of the congregation, with the hope of increasing church attendance and membership. An organizing outreach focuses on the interests and concerns of neighbors, intending to identify issues that the congregation, along with its neighbors, might choose to address through collective public action.

PICO   See "Faith in Action."

Public Meeting   A large gathering to which public officials and others who hold public power are invited to hear testimonies regarding an issue that the organization intends to impact. Leaders focus on turning out impressive numbers of participants in order to show policy makers what kind of power the organization can wield. Besides testimonies, public actions also include the stating of expectations the organization has with regard to the issue, and the opportunity for policy makers to commit to enacting the changes sought by the organization.

Socratic Method   A teaching tool attributed to the philosopher Socrates, designed to develop students' critical thinking skills. It works well when engaging a large group of students in a discussion, using probing or provocative questions to get at the heart of one's subject matter.

Synod   A term used by the Evangelical Lutheran Church in America (ELCA) to identify its sixty-five regional offices around the United States. Each synod is staffed by a locally elected bishop, who, along with other synod staff, oversees the operation of numerous individual congregations and ministries within its designated territory.

Recommended Reading

Bretherton, Luke. *Resurrecting Democracy: Faith, Citizenship, and the Politics of a Common Life.* New York: Cambridge University Press, 2015.

Condor, Tim, and Dan Rhodes. *Organizing Church: Grassroots Practices for Embodying Change in Your Congregation, Your Community, and Our World.* St. Louis: Chalice Press, 2017.

Evans, Sara M., and Harry C. Boyt. *Free Spaces: The Sources of Democratic Change in America.* New York: Harper and Row, 1986.

Gecan, Michael. *Going Public: An Organizer's Guide to Citizen Action.* New York: Anchor Books, 2004.

Jacobsen, Dennis. *Doing Justice: Congregations and Community Organizing,* second edition. Minneapolis: Fortress Press, 2017.

Linthicum, Robert. *Transforming Power: Biblical Strategies for Making a Difference in Your Community.* Downers Grove, IL: Intervarsity Press, 2003.

Neumark, Heidi. *Breathing Space: A Spiritual Journey in the South Bronx.* Boston: Beacon Press, 2004.

Orr, Marion. *Transforming the City: Community Organizing and the Challenge of Political Change.* Lawrence: University Press of Kansas, 2007.

Ransby, Barbara. *Ella Baker and the Black Freedom Movement: A Radical Democratic Vision.* Chapel Hill: University of North Carolina Press, 2003.

Rivera, Ray. *Liberty to the Captives: Our Call to Minister in a Captive World.* Grand Rapids: Eerdmans, 2012.

Salvatierra, Alexia, and Peter Heltzel. *Faith-Rooted Organizing: Mobilizing the Church in Service to the World.* Downers Grove, IL: Intervarsity Press, 2014.

Slessarev-Jamir, Helen. *Prophetic Activism: Progressive Religious Justice Movements in Contemporary America.* New York: New York University Press, 2011.

Snarr, C. Melissa. *All You that Labor: Religion and Ethics in the Living Wage Movement.* New York: New York University Press, 2004.

Stout, Jeffrey. *Blessed Are the Organized: Grassroots Democracy in America.* Princeton, NJ: Princeton University Press, 2010.

Whitman, Gordon. *Stand Up! How to Get Involved, Speak Out, and Win in a World on Fire.* Oakland, CA: Berrett-Koehler Publishers, Inc., 2018.

Wood, Richard L., and Brad R. Fulton. *A Shared Future: Faith-Based Organizing for Racial Equity and Ethical Democracy.* Chicago: University of Chicago Press, 2015.

Woodley, Randy. *Shalom and the Community of Creation: An Indigenous Vision.* Prophetic Christian Series, vol. 2. Grand Rapids: Eerdmans, 2012.

Index

Midwest Academy, 13
Morales, Ricardo Levins, 100

Nathan Cummings Foundation, 62
National Baptist Convention, USA, 59, 60, 123
National Day Laborer Organizing Network, 65
Nehemiah public action, 55
Nelson, Myrna, 85, 104, 109–11, 128, 131–32
Norton, John, 135
Ntosake, 19–22, 84–85, 138

one-to-one, 27, 31, 37–38, 41, 47, 49, 63, 67, 70, 73, 104, 148–50
Orfield, Myron, 87–88, 105
organizing cycle, 102–14
organizing network(s), xiii, 2–3, 5, 11, 13, 27, 53, 55, 59–61, 72, 73, 75, 80, 84–91, 93, 95, 113–14, 147–49
Organizing for Mission Cohort, 68–71
outreach, 106, 147, 150

People's Action, 12
PICO. *See* Faith in Action
powell, john, 93
public action, 2, 55, 61, 72, 87–88, 109–12, 115, 134, 150
public arena, 14, 21–22, 27–28, 39, 50, 60–61, 66, 82, 85, 88, 93, 102

race/racism, 24, 69, 71, 92–94, 100, 116, 129, 137, 139, 148, 149
Rahab (biblical character), 124–25
Reconciling in Christ (RIC), 66
Reed, Melissa, 24–25, 37, 47–49, 52, 56, 76–77, 119, 124, 137
Reform California, 64–66
research, 32, 53, 64–65, 101, 104–7, 109, 114

sacred texts, 1, 4, 14, 61–62, 118, 138
Safe Return, 32, 94
Sarah (biblical character), 128–29

Schmitt, Jay, 30
Schrantz, Doran, 10, 29, 55–56, 82, 90, 92–93, 126–27, 132
schulte, eva, 89, 122, 123, 125, 127–28, 137
self-interest, 10, 17–20, 28–29, 38, 40–41, 44–45, 52, 66, 70, 84, 86, 90, 130, 134, 138, 149
Seminary Leadership Program, 62
sexual identity, 46, 66–68, 116, 139, 149
Shaw, William, 59
Sheba, Queen of (biblical character), 131
Sobocienski, Meghan, dedication, 68–70, 88–89, 98, 106–7, 112–13, 114, 120, 123
subsidiarity, 89–90

Tabitha (biblical character), 121
training, xiii, 3, 9, 12–14, 17–21, 26–33, 37, 41, 45, 60–64, 66–67, 71, 73–74, 81, 83–88, 91–92, 95, 99–100, 125, 127, 134–35, 138, 147, 149
turnout, 12, 51–52, 55, 86, 88, 90, 109, 111, 150
Twiss, Pamela, 10, 12–13, 18, 27–28, 32–33, 84, 87–88, 122, 126

Union for Reform Judaism, 60
Unitarian Universalist Association (UUA), 11, 37, 46, 59–60, 71–94, 114–15, 122, 144

Vazquez, Bianca, 69
Veatch Program, 73–74
vocation, 19, 32, 50, 56, 121, 130

Walker, Tamisha, 32, 53–54, 81–82, 93–94, 104–5, 134–35
Wellstone, Paul, 104
Wiley, Leah, 40, 55, 86–87, 95, 102, 125–26
Williamson, Marianne, 138

About the Author

The Rev. **Susan Engh** was born in Chicago and raised in its northwest suburbs. She received her Bachelor of Arts degree from Augustana University and her Master of Divinity from Luther Seminary. She served for sixteen years as a parish pastor at ELCA congregations in Minneapolis and Excelsior, Minnesota, then became a full-time faith-based community organizer for ISAIAH of Minnesota. Since 2007 she has served as Program Director for Congregation-based Organizing for the Evangelical Lutheran Church in America. She is also a clergy consultant to the Gamaliel national organizing network. Susan lives with her husband Michael in Minneapolis. They have two adult children and two grandchildren.

Kim Bobo is the Co-Executive Director of the Virginia Interfaith Center for Public Policy. In 1996 she founded Interfaith Worker Justice, and served as its Executive Director for twenty years. She is the author of *Wage Theft in America: Why Millions of Working Americans Are Not Getting Paid—and What We Can Do About It* (2011) and *Lives Matter: A Handbook for Christian Organizing* (1986), among other publications.

CPSIA information can be obtained
at www.ICGtesting.com
Printed in the USA
LVHW041646031121
702359LV00011B/1811